AUGUSTAN SATIRE
INTENTION AND IDIOM
IN ENGLISH POETRY
1660-1750

Un classique . . . c'est d'abord un inventeur,
c'est un explorateur

AUGUSTAN SATIRE

INTENTION AND IDIOM
IN ENGLISH POETRY
1660–1750

BY

IAN JACK

OXFORD
AT THE CLARENDON PRESS

Oxford University Press, Amen House, London E.C.4

GLASGOW   NEW YORK   TORONTO   MELBOURNE   WELLINGTON
BOMBAY   CALCUTTA   MADRAS   KARACHI   KUALA LUMPUR
CAPE TOWN   IBADAN   NAIROBI   ACCRA

FIRST EDITION 1952

REPRINTED LITHOGRAPHICALLY IN GREAT BRITAIN
AT THE UNIVERSITY PRESS, OXFORD
FROM CORRECTED SHEETS OF THE FIRST EDITION
1957, 1961

PREFACE

A RECENT critic has said that 'it is better to be spurred to acquire scholarship because you enjoy the poetry, than to suppose that you enjoy the poetry because you have acquired the scholarship'. Perhaps this may serve as a comment on my approach to these great Augustan satires. Enthusiasm led me to literary history.

In writing this book I have incurred many debts. I feel fortunate to have joined the large company of those who have profited from the kindness and scholarship of Professor Nichol Smith, who read part of my study in an earlier form and helped me constantly with advice and encouragement. Mr. Hugh Macdonald has been characteristically generous with his time and his remarkable knowledge of the seventeenth century. Miss Helen Gardner, whose lectures on Dryden I found most stimulating, made suggestions from which I have tried to profit. Professor Rosemond Tuve encouraged me during one of those periods of depression that are the student's occupational disease: in *Elizabethan and Metaphysical Imagery* I have found a constant source of ideas. Col. C. H. Wilkinson was generous enough to make me a present of his discovery that D'Urfey's *The Progress of Honesty* has interesting resemblances to *Absalom and Achitophel*. Mr. Harold F. Brooks has allowed me to quote from his unpublished thesis on John Oldham.

I also wish to thank the trustees of the Carnegie Trust and the Cross Trust for the generous award of a Research Scholarship which made possible my years at Merton.

Two obligations are even harder to assess: that to the scholar to whom this book is dedicated, who first interested me in the Augustan age; and that to my wife, whose book on Defoe would have been completed sooner but for the ungrudging assistance she has given me whenever I have been in need of it.

My thanks are due to the editor of the *Times Literary Supplement* for permission to make use of passages which first appeared in his pages.

Finally, a separate page not being available, I should like to conclude by saying that this book is dedicated

TO

GEORGE KITCHIN

TEACHER

AND FRIEND

I. J.

BRASENOSE COLLEGE, OXFORD
August 1951

CONTENTS

ABBREVIATIONS

E.-C.	*The Works of Alexander Pope*, ed. W. Elwin and W. J. Courthope.
E.L.H.	*Journal of English Literary History.*
H.L.Q.	*Huntington Library Quarterly.*
J.E.G.P.	*Journal of English and Germanic Philology.*
M.L.N.	*Modern Language Notes.*
M.P.	*Modern Philology.*
P.M.L.A.	*Publications of the Modern Language Association of America.*
P.Q.	*Philological Quarterly.*
R.E.S.	*Review of English Studies.*
S.P.	*Studies in Philology.*
Spence	*Anecdotes, Observations, and Characters, of Books and Men.* Collected by Joseph Spence, ed. S. W. Singer (1820).
Spingarn	*Critical Essays of the Seventeenth Century*, ed. J. E. Spingarn.
S.-S.	*The Works of John Dryden*, ed. Walter Scott, rev. George Saintsbury.

INTRODUCTION

In this study I have examined the style of certain of the most representative poems written in England between the Restoration and the middle of the eighteenth century. By relating them to the critical theory of the time I have tried to help the modern reader to approach them with some understanding of what the poet was trying to do and how he set about it.

Although Augustan poetry is more popular today than it was in the nineteenth century, modern critics seldom submit to the discipline necessary for a full historical understanding. In particular the question of the different 'kinds' and the various 'levels of style' has been little investigated. After mentioning the importance of the theory of the kinds, for example, the author of one of the most useful of recent studies of Pope sketches the general requirements in epic, dramatic (primarily tragic), and pastoral poetry, and dismisses the matter in these words: 'So much for Pope's connections with and views upon, the principal *genres* of his time.'[1] Since Pope did not complete one epic or tragedy, while his *Pastorals*, however remarkable, are 'prentice work, this seems rather perfunctory. Are we to conclude that Pope's major poems do not require interpretation in terms of the kinds in which they are written?

Fortunately other critics have devoted some attention to these questions. Professor Mark Van Doren's book *The Poetry of John Dryden* and the writings of Professor Tillotson and Professor Sutherland are among the most notable attempts to push back the frontiers of our ignorance. But there still seems to be room for a close study of the idioms in which a number of specific Augustan poems are written.

My object has been to trace the implications of Pope's remark when he praised Dryden in these terms: 'Dryden

[1] A. Warren, *Alexander Pope as Critic and Humanist* (1929), p. 75.

always uses proper language; lively, natural, and fitted to the subject. It is scarce ever too high, or too low.'[1]

Any attempt to examine English poetry between 1660 and 1750 must be extremely general or extremely selective. Since my object was minute stylistic analysis, I was obliged to be extremely selective. And since I wished to avoid byways and concentrate on the central poems of the period, several of the poems selected themselves. To have omitted *MacFlecknoe*, *Absalom and Achitophel*, *The Rape of the Lock*, *The Dunciad*, or *The Vanity of Human Wishes* would have been absurd.

In choosing other poems to make up the complement of my study I had again a choice to make. I could choose what seemed to me the best poems of the period, independent of genre or general character; or I could limit my selection in some way. There was little difficulty in deciding. I noticed that the poems I had already chosen were all, in spite of wide differences, satires; and I found that several of the other poems which seemed most eligible were also satirical. It was clear that my study would become more manageable if it were confined to satirical poetry.

Since it was an axiom of critical theory in this period that 'in every design which a man deliberately undertakes, the end he proposes is the first thing in his mind, and that by which he governs the whole work, and all its parts',[2] one cannot analyse the style of any Augustan poem without first asking what the poet's object was in writing it, and to what poetic kind it belongs. As I learned more about the way in which these poets approached their task I found it more and more important, if any sort of balance was to be maintained, to deal with other things than idiom itself—considerations which came before the choice of style, and helped to determine it. In examining each poem I was obliged to deal summarily with the poet's aim and the nature of his material.

[1] *Anecdotes, Observations, and Characters, of Books and Men. Collected . . . by . . . Joseph Spence*, ed. S. W. Singer (1820), p. 281.

[2] *A General View of the Epick Poem . . . Extracted from Bossu*, prefixed to Pope's *Odyssey*, Sect. II.

I

'THE SILVER AGE OF THE EUROPEAN RENAISSANCE'

They obtain'd first to write well, and then custome made it easie and a habit.

BEN JONSON[1]

For the literary historian 'the silver age of the . . . European Renaissance'[2] is the period between the civil wars and the middle of the eighteenth century. It was in these years that the ideals produced by the inter-action of medievalism and the vigorous classical and Continental influences of the new age last afforded the background of critical theory which supported poets in their endeavours. The literary patriotism of the Renaissance flared up when Dryden described himself, with a proud humility, as 'a Man, who have done my best to improve the Language, & Especially the Poetry'.[3] And when Pope defined the task of the poet as the expression of 'what oft was thought, but ne'er so well express'd'[4] he was not, as has often been suggested, uttering a barren half-truth characteristic of an age lacking in originality, but simply repeating a Renaissance common-place to which Spenser, Shakespeare, and Milton would have given their assent. Pope's belief that 'no writing is good that does not tend to better mankind some way or other'[5] is not more clearly in the tradition of Renaissance orthodoxy than this definition. His constant ambition to be 'correct', which

---

[1] *Timber, or Discoveries*, in *Critical Essays of the Seventeenth Century*, ed. J. E. Spingarn (1908–9), i. 32.

[2] A. N. Whitehead, *Adventures of Ideas* (ed. of 1934), p. 6. Quoted by Basil Willey in *The Eighteenth Century Background* (1940), p. 1.

[3] *The Letters of John Dryden*, ed. Charles E. Ward (1942), p. 123. Cf. a letter to Dryden from Dennis, when he had heard that Dryden was planning a translation of Virgil: 'We know that whatever you undertake must prove Glorious to England, and tho the French may meet with Success in the Field, by you we are sure to Conquer them. . . . In a Combat of Wit, the more Humane Contention, and the more Glorious Quarrel, Merit will be always sure to prevail . . . Boileau and Racine will be forced to submit to you. . . .' Ibid., p. 66.

[4] *An Essay on Criticism*, l. 298.   [5] Spence, p. 203.

seemed to a Romantic generation the last excess of arid
pedantry, was informed by the same excitement that animated Spenser and Milton, the sense that there was one
respect in which English poetry still lagged behind the
literatures of Greece and Rome.

II

'The universal fault of our literature', Hopkins wrote to
a friend, '[is] its weakness [in] rhetoric. The strictly poetical
insight and inspiration of our poetry seems to me to be of
the very finest . . . but its rhetoric is inadequate—seldom
firstrate, mostly only just sufficient, sometimes even below
par. By rhetoric I mean all the common and teachable element in literature, what grammar is to speech.'[1]

This censure falls more heavily on Romantic and post-
Romantic poetry in England than on that written earlier.
In the long period of the Renaissance the deficiency in 'the
common and teachable element in literature' was much less
marked. The modern reader of Ben Jonson and Milton
notices the deliberateness with which they set out to gain
their effects, and their skilful adaptation of means to the
end desired. Indeed it is in the primary importance that it
assigned to *intention* that the heart of Renaissance poetics
must be sought. No absolute distinction was drawn between
poetry and other sorts of writing. Poetry and oratory were
sister arts.

The relations between them were discussed in the lectures
delivered by the first Oxford Professor of Poetry, Joseph
Trapp, at the beginning of the eighteenth century.

Another Question may possibly be ask'd [Trapp remarked], and
deservedly too . . . how far Poetry and Oratory agree, and wherein
they differ. To give a direct Answer to this, we say, that Eloquence is
common to both; Eloquence, therefore, ought to be consider'd as twofold; that of Oratory, and that of Poetry. Those Things that come

---

[1] *The Correspondence of Gerard Manley Hopkins and Richard Watson Dixon*, ed. Claude
Colleer Abbott (1935), p. 141.

under the Title of Eloquence in general, relate to both Arts; such as, Topicks of Praise, whether of Persons, Facts, or Things; Topicks of Exhortation, Congratulation, Consolation, and the like, with which the Orator, as well as the Poet, excites Anger, Love, Pity, and all other Passions. Both observe alike a proper Decorum of Manners, according to Age, Fortune, and Condition of Life. Ardent Expressions, and lively Thoughts, are the Embellishments of both. In both the Diction is elevated, or familiar, grave, florid, or strong, as Occasion serves. For all these Things . . . are Branches of Eloquence in general, are drawn from the same Heads of Invention, and illustrated by Examples fetch'd from Orators or Poets.[1]

The differences between oratory and poetry—principally metre and 'Fiction', according to Trapp—are not in question here. What is relevant is Trapp's insistence on the common ground shared by poets and orators. Like a speech, a poem must be written with attention to the effect it will have on its audience. It is not so much an expression of emotion as a calculated attempt to arouse emotion in its readers.[2] A lampooning satire, for example, is not necessarily an expression of hatred (if it is merely that it will hardly be a good satire): it is an attempt to arouse hatred towards its subject in the mind of the public. When Valéry said that a poem was 'une sorte de machine'[3] he was merely restating, in provocative form, a fundamental truth which would have been acknowledged by Dryden or Pope.

III

In one matter, at least, Renaissance poets and critics were profoundly empirical. If a man wanted to write a poem praising his mistress or blaming his enemy, describing a beautiful scene or inviting a friend to dine, what was more

---

[1] Trapp's lectures were published in Latin in two vols. in 1711 and 1715, under the title of *Praelectiones Poeticae*. My quotations are from the English translation of. 1742 (*Lectures on Poetry . . . With additional Notes*), p. 34.

[2]   Here be your Language lofty, there more light,
        Your Rethorick with your Poetry unite.

John Wilmot, Earl of Rochester: *An Allusion to the Tenth Satyr of the First Book of Horace* (*c.* 1677–9?), ll. 24–25. Spingarn, ii. 283. (My italics.)

[3] 'Poésie et pensée abstraite', in *Variétés V* (24e éd., 1945), p. 159.

reasonable—they argued—than that he should inquire how earlier poets had done the same thing?

'To the Antient Greecs and Latins', a critic wrote in 1675, 'the Modern Poets of all Nations and for several Ages have acknowledged themselves beholding for those, both Precepts and examples, which have been thought conducing to the perfection of Poetry.'[1] The so-called 'doctrine' of the 'kinds' was simply an attempt by critics to make the experience of these classical poets available to their successors. The word 'doctrine', however, is misleading; the theory was much less rigid than has often been supposed, allowing of great variations within the kind. The Renaissance habit of ranking the kinds in a hierarchy analogous to that of the state has also led to widespread distrust. Just as the social hierarchy was traced from the prince through the nobility down to the common people, so the realm of Poetry had its own 'degrees', from Epic, the Prince of all the kinds, down to the lowest species of all, 'from Homer to the *Anthologia*, from Virgil to Martial and Owen's Epigrams . . . that is, from the top to the bottom of all poetry'.[2]

This ranking of the kinds has made little appeal to critics of an age when the social hierarchy has all but disappeared. We are sceptical now about the inherent superiority and dignity of certain subjects and poetic aims, and prefer to make the hazardous attempt to weigh the worth of a poem simply by the poet's performance, without troubling about the importance of the kind to which it belongs. But since the ranking of the kinds in a hierarchy is no inseparable part of the belief that poetry may be divided into kinds, it should not prejudice us against the whole idea. The belief in the kinds made for clarity in the poet's planning, economy in his execution of what he planned, and the possibility of some sort of cogency in the business of criticism.

The idea of the heroic poem, in particular, was central in all discussions of poetry from the late sixteenth century until

---

1 Edward Phillips, Preface to *Theatrum Poetarum*, in Spingarn, ii. 264.
2 *Essays of John Dryden*, ed. W. P. Ker (1900), ii. 27.

the middle of the eighteenth. No manifestation of the continuing Renaissance tradition in the Augustan period is more noteworthy. Throughout his life Pope, no less than Spenser, Milton, and Dryden, shared the Renaissance ambition to write one supreme poem comparable to the great classical epics. 'The idea that I have had for an Epic poem, of late', he told Spence in the last few months of his life, 'turns wholly on civil and ecclesiastical government.' The sketch of the fable was as follows: 'The hero is a prince who establishes an empire. That prince is our Brutus from Troy; and the scene of the establishment, England. The plan of government is much like our old original plan; supposed so much earlier: and the religion, introduced by him, is the belief of one God, and the doctrines of morality.'[1] The similarity between Pope's proposed epic and the epics planned in the Elizabethan Age, in general design, action, and 'end', is very striking.

It is not only in the study of epics that the idea of the heroic poem is important. It acted as a centre of discussion much as 'la poésie pure' did in France a few decades ago. Since the heroic poem was the poem *par excellence*, a poet would remember Homer and Virgil and borrow from them hints for the style and structure of his own composition even when he was not attempting to write an epic. Without the idea of the heroic poem in the background five at least of the 'satires' examined in this study could not have been written in the form in which we know them.

Hudibras, MacFlecknoe, Absalom and Achitophel, The Rape of the Lock, and *The Dunciad* are evidence that belief in the kinds did not necessarily stultify originality. None of them belongs to a genre with a classical prototype. In *The Art of Sinking in Poetry* Pope satirized those who 'by the light of their own Genius . . . attempt upon *new Models*';[2] yet in two

---

[1] p. 288.

[2] Chap. I, *ad fin.*—Pope told Spence that '*The Profound*, though written in so ludicrous a way, may be very well worth reading seriously, as an art of rhetoric' (p. 176). I have taken him at his word. My references are to the edition of Edna Leake Steeves (New York, 1952).

It must be noted, however, that throughout it is primarily bad writers *in the more elevated*

of his most celebrated satires he wrote poems different from anything to be found in Homer or Virgil or Horace. This does not mean that these poems were created in a vacuum, however, or in contempt of the older kinds. They were developments in which a modern poet blended originality with tradition to create a poem adapted to his precise purpose.

The style of a poem was expected to suit the poet's subject and the kind which he was practising. A Renaissance critic was giving high praise if he said that a poet's style was 'constantly accommodated to his subject, either high or low'.[1] It is because Dryden wanted his work to be judged by this criterion of decorum that the main subject of the prefaces to most of his poems, flattery apart, is the kind which he has tried to exemplify, and the style which he has chosen as appropriate. The preface to *Religio Laici* is typical: 'If any one be so lamentable a Critique as to require the Smoothness, the Numbers, and the Turn of Heroique Poetry in this Poem; I must tell him, that, if he has not read *Horace*, I have studied him, and hope the style of his Epistles is not ill imitated here.' In the same spirit Young prefixed an *Essay on Lyric Poetry* to a collection of his odes. 'How imperfect soever my own composition may be', he wrote, 'yet am I willing to speak a word or two of the nature of Lyric Poetry: to shew that I have, at least, some idea of perfection in that kind of poem in which I am engaged; and that I do not think myself poet enough entirely to rely on inspiration for my success in it.'[2]

kinds that Pope is satirizing. Some of the advice ironically given to the would-be heroic writer is excellent advice for the satirist—for example, the recommendation of 'low', degrading comparisons.

Conversely, when Pope remarks, in the *Imitations of Horace, Satires*, ii. i—

Verse-man or Prose-man, term me which you will (l. 64)

—he is referring only to his work in the low genre of epistolary satire. He would not have referred to *The Rape of the Lock* or *Eloisa to Abelard* as the work of a 'Prose-man'.

[1] Dryden on Horace, *Essays*, ii. 78. Cowley began to write 'a Discourse concerning Style' in which 'he had design'd to give an account of the proper sorts of writing that were fit for all manner of Arguments, to compare the perfections and imperfections of the Authors of Antiquity with those of this present Age, and to deduce all down to the particular use of the English Genius and Language'. (Sprat's *Life*, in Spingarn, ii. 142.) Cowley died before he had made much progress with this plan. Two works with roughly similar aims are Sir Thomas Pope Blount's critical anthology, *De Re Poetica* (1694), and Trapp's *Lectures on Poetry*.

[2] *Works* (1774), vi. 111.

When Pope read a poem one of the matters which he considered most critically was whether the level of style had been well chosen. He considered that nothing in Homer

seems to have been more commonly mistaken than the just Pitch of his Style: Some of his Translators having swell'd into Fustian in a proud Confidence of the *Sublime*: others sunk into *Flatness*, in a cold and timorous Notion of *Simplicity*.[1]

The true aspirant to Dullness

is to consider himself as a *Grotesque* Painter, whose Works would be spoil'd by an Imitation of Nature, or Uniformity of Design. He is to mingle Bits of the most various, or discordant kinds, Landscape, History, Portraits, Animals, and connect them with a great deal of *Flourishing*, by *Heads* or *Tails*, as it shall please his Imagination, and contribute to his principal End, which is to glare by strong Oppositions of Colours, and surprize by Contrariety of Images.[2]

There was no aspect of the art of poetry to which Pope paid more attention in his own work than this matter of maintaining a just level of style.

After writing a poem [he told Spence] one should correct it all over, with one single view at a time. Thus for language; if an elegy; 'these lines are very good, but are not they of too heroical a strain?' and so *vice versa*. It appears very plainly . . . that Homer did this; and it is yet plainer that Virgil did so, from the distinct styles he uses in his three sorts of poems. . . . So constant an effect could not be the effect of chance.[3]

Pope developed his perceptiveness of the texture of verse to a remarkable degree, and even ventured to find fault with Virgil for occasional negligence. 'Though Virgil, in his pastorals, has sometimes six or eight lines together that are epic', he once remarked, 'I have been so scrupulous as scarce ever to admit above two together, even in the Messiah.'[4] A modern reader who aspires to read Pope with

---

[1] Preface to the *Iliad*, para. xxv (*Prose Works*, ed. Ault (1936), i. 245).

[2] *The Art of Sinking in Poetry*, ch. v. (Pope is remembering the opening lines of Horace's 'Art of Poetry'.)   [3] Spence, pp. 23–24.

[4] Ibid., p. 312. Cf. *The Letters of Sir Thomas Fitzosborne, on Several Subjects* [by William Melmoth], fourth ed. 1754, Letter xxxvii, a.f.

' "His eyes shall weep the folly of his tongue":
tho a good line in itself, is much too solemn and tragical for the undisturbed pleasantry of Horace.' (My italics.)

something of the same understanding as a well-informed contemporary must labour to develop a keen awareness of the different levels of idiom.

IV

In making this attempt the modern reader will be trying to recover one of the principal benefits of a conservative seventeenth-century education. During the Augustan period the reaction against the old formal education in favour of a more obviously useful sort of learning was gathering force. Yet the old type of education was still usual, particularly in the public schools and the better grammar schools—and it was there that youths aspiring to a literary career were normally educated. In spite of men like Defoe and Locke 'the old talkative *Arts*'[1] so prominent in the earlier part of the Renaissance still formed the core of a sound education.[2] Since 'the Muses seldom vouchsafe their favours, where there is not a preparation suitable to their dignity and greatness',[3] to equip a boy to speak and write persuasively remained a primary object of the teacher.[4]

The humblest instruments in such an education were the works of the classical rhetoricians, Aristotle, Cicero, Horace,[5]

[1] Sprat's *History of the Royal-Society of London*, p. 324. When the passage is not in Spingarn, my references are to the 'corrected' second edition of 1702.

[2] Cf. Davenant: 'Yong men, as if they were not quite deliver'd from Childhood, whose first exercise is Language, imagine [Wit] consists in the Musick of words, and beleeve they are made wise by refining their Speech above the vulgar Dialect. . . .' *Preface to Gondibert*, in Spingarn, ii. 21–22.

[3] The Honourable Edward Howard, in the preface to *The Women's Conquest* (1671).

[4] Several studies of the part played by rhetoric in Renaissance education have appeared recently.

While such works as Donald Lemen Clark's *John Milton at St. Paul's School. A Study of Ancient Rhetoric in English Renaissance Education* (1948) have their value, however, any close correlation between a poet's education and his work is (as Clark points out) dangerous. It is the general attitude to language that is important.

Cf. Prior's remark in his *Heads for a Treatise Upon Learning*: 'Those bred at Westminster Schole . . . gained probably from their being used very Young to what Dr. Sprat calls the Genius of that place which is to Verses made Extempore, and Declamations composed in very few hours, in which sort of Exercises when Children they take from whence so ever they can, which when Men they repay with great Interest. . . .' (*Dialogues of the Dead*, ed. Waller (1907), p. 184.)

[5] 'If any of them hath acquired a credit . . . superior to the rest, it is, perhaps, the *following work*', Richard Hurd wrote in his introduction to Horace's poem. (*Q. Horatii Flacci Epistolae ad Pisones, et Augustum*, ed. of 1766, i. i.)

and Quintilian. The essentially practical spirit in which these books were studied is clear from Pope's commendation of one of the most used of all:

> In grave Quintilian's copious work, we find
> The justest rules, and clearest method join'd:
> Thus useful arms in magazines we place,
> All rang'd in order, and dispos'd with grace,
> But less to please the eye, than arm the hand,
> Still fit for use, and ready at command.[1]

While a schoolboy would normally know parts of these books or of modern rhetorics based on them, however, the best teachers insisted that a first-hand knowledge of the works of the greatest writers was more valuable than any study of rhetoric books. When Joseph Trapp, addressing an audience which had recently left school for university, protested against 'those Books of Rhetorick that are usually read in Schools . . . so full of dry, logical Definitions',[2] he was not proving himself a rebel 'ahead of his age', but merely expressing an orthodox neo-classical belief which can be traced back to the sixteenth century at least. 'A Knowledge of these Things will be much better arrived at by Experience, than Precept', he continued. 'And every one that is conversant with the best Authors, that reads them with Understanding, and true Relish, cannot but be acquainted with all the Figures of Speech, and the Art of using them, tho' he never heard so much as their Names, or their Definitions.'[3] Perhaps Trapp was remembering a passage in the *Life of Cowley* where Sprat remarks that Cowley 'was wont to relate that he had this defect in his memory . . . that his Teachers could never bring it to retain the ordinary Rules of Grammar. However, he supply'd that want, by conversing with the Books themselves from whence those Rules had been drawn. That no doubt was a better way, though much more difficult.'[4]

---

[1] *An Essay on Criticism*, ll. 670–5.   [2] p. 53.
[3] p. 54.   [4] Spingarn, ii. 121.

Sprat's account of Cowley's education may stand as a statement of the ideal of the time:

The first beginning of his Studies was a familiarity with the most solid and unaffected Authors of Antiquity, which he fully digested not only in his memory but his judgment. By this advantage he learnt nothing while a Boy that he needed to forget or forsake when he came to be a man. His mind was rightly season'd at first, and he had nothing to do but still to proceed on the same Foundation on which he began.[1]

At a time when the study of rhetoric flourished as it still did in the Augustan age, even a man who had the same difficulty as Cowley in remembering the names of the figures of speech read the great classical and modern writers with the help of the lenses which rhetoric provided. A modern schoolboy reads Virgil with little awareness of the subtleties of his art: his predecessor of the seventeenth century had a great advantage. Even a poet like Pope, whose early education had been informal, lived in an age so steeped in the rhetorical tradition that he could not have read a page without being influenced by this current of interpretation and criticism.

Throughout the Augustan period translation from the classical languages into English was of fundamental importance in all sound education. 'I remember', Dryden wrote of Persius's Third Satire when he was an old man, 'I translated this Satyr, when I was a *Kings-Scholar* at *Westminster* School, for a *Thursday* Nights *Exercise*; and believe that it, and many other of my *Exercises* of this nature, in *English Verse*, are still in the Hands of my *Learned Master*, the Reverend Doctor *Busby*.'[2] Verse was often translated into verse, and a certain measure of elegance was demanded even from a schoolboy's version: 'I admire some men should perpetually stumble in a way so easy', Dryden once complained, 'and inverting the order of their words, constantly close their lines with verbs, which though commended some-

---

[1] Spingarn, ii. 121.
[2] Note appended to the 'Argument' of Dryden's translation.

.times in writing Latin, yet we were whipt at Westminster if we used it twice together.'[1]

Imitations of the best Latin writers were expected at school and university, as well as translations. The works of Donne, Herbert, Vaughan, Cowley, Addison, and Johnson contain evidence that this often led to a lifelong habit of writing Latin verse,[2] and there can be little doubt that the concept of the different kinds of poetry owed a good deal to this practice. It is one thing to read Virgil or Horace so as to be able to construe with accuracy, and another to read with understanding enough to be capable of writing a passable imitation. A man who had been censured at school for writing 'too high for an epistle' when he tried to imitate Horace, retained throughout his life a keen awareness of the different levels of style. He tended to read the classical writers more attentively than he would otherwise have done, asking himself: How does he do it? How is this effect achieved?

Imitation was a much more dignified activity than most people think it today.[3] Whereas we tend to think of a poem as self-expression, an outpouring of the personality more or less controlled, the men of the Renaissance regarded it partly, as has been remarked, as a piece of writing designed to move the reader in a certain way, and partly as an artifact, an example of fine craftsmanship. No doubt a great writer finally evolves a style of his own (or rather a number of styles, for the different genres he practises); but he must

---

[1] *Essays*, i. 6.

[2] Leicester Bradner's *Musae Anglicanae: A History of Anglo-Latin Poetry 1500–1925* (1940) is a useful guide. Even at school original Latin poems were expected from pupils on such set themes as the Gunpowder Plot. In his unpublished D.Phil. thesis on John Oldham (which I have been allowed to read through his courtesy and that of Mr. Hugh Macdonald), Mr. H. F. Brooks remarks that in 1678 the poet's pupils 'wrote execrable verses "On Gunpowder treason plot", "On the powder plot" and "On the Late Plot", with opening lines apparently set by their master himself' (p. lvi). (These may be found in Bodl. MS. Rawlinson Poet. 123, pp. 255, 263.) The habit of setting the Gunpowder Plot as a subject for verses lasted a long time: the influence of such compositions may perhaps be detected in *Absalom and Achitophel*. Cf. p. 58 n. 5.

[3] 'You observe, I am a mere *imitator of Homer, Horace, Boileau, Garth*, &c. (which I have the less cause to be ashamed of, since they were imitators of one another).' Pope's *Letter to a Noble Lord* (*Works*, ed. Elwin-Courthope (1871–89), v. 438).

begin by imitating, as closely as he can, the styles of the best masters of each kind. Spence remarks that Pope 'had the greatest compass, in imitating styles, that I ever knew in any man: and he had it partly from his method of instructing himself, after he was out of the hands of his bad masters, which was, at first, almost wholly by imitation'.[1] It was no more ridiculous or contemptible for a poet to imitate Virgil or Horace than for a craftsman to imitate a master in the realms of architecture or furniture-making.[2] When a man can make a table that might pass for a Sheraton—to paraphrase the Renaissance attitude—he may be in a position to make a fine piece of furniture after a design of his own.[3] In the necessary period of tutelage no treason against the personality is involved.

The prominent part played by imitation in an orthodox seventeenth-century education has consequences apt to mislead the modern reader. Just as a schoolboy set to write a copy of Latin verses was told which classical poet to imitate, the choice being determined by the genre he was to attempt, so a man sitting down to write a poem often used the work of some earlier writer as a model. In every major poem Pope wrote, for example, he had before him the example of some great classical poet. This does not mean that he imitated him slavishly, but that the general level of his style was modelled on that of the classical writer. His satires are, many of them, 'allusions' to specific satires of Horace; the *Essay on Criticism* is modelled on Horace's *Art of Poetry*; while Lucretius furnished the model for the *Essay on Man*.[4]

It is clear at the outset, therefore, that any attempt to trace the development of a poet's style or the influence of one poet on another is as dangerous in the Augustan age as in

[1] p. 168.

[2] Cf. Dryden's remark that 'The *Materia Poetica* is as common to all writers, as the *Materia Medica* to all physicians'. (Preface to *Don Sebastian*, in Malone's ed. of the *Prose Works* (1800), ii. 190.)

[3] 'My first taking to imitating was not out of vanity, but humility', Pope told Spence (p. 278): 'I saw how defective my own things were; and endeavoured to mend my manner, by copying good strokes from others.'

[4] See *E.-C.* ii. 273.

the earlier part of the Renaissance.[1] A poet's style varies according to the sort of poem he is writing, and the influences which come into play depend on the nature of the work. As Virgil was the best model for heroic poetry, and Horace for epistolary satire, so amongst English poets Ben Jonson was the model for certain sorts of epigram and epitaph and Donne, on occasion, for the more extended type of funeral elegy.[2] The naïvety of modern criticism has been very evident in attempts to approach these problems. No aspect of the idiom of a Renaissance poem can be investigated without a full understanding of the demands of decorum.[3] Any critic who thinks of inquiring into the survival of elements of 'Metaphysical Wit' in the Augustan period, for example, would do well to consider the following passage from *The Art of Sinking in Poetry* before he begins:

Nothing is more evident than that divers Persons, no other way remarkable, have each a strong Disposition to the Formation of some particular Trope or Figure. . . . Now each man applying his whole Time and Genius upon his particular Figure, would doubtless attain to Perfection; and when each became incorporated and sworn into the Society . . . a Poet or Orator would have no more to do, but to send to the particular Traders in each Kind; to the *Metaphorist* for his *Allegories*, to the *Simile-maker* for his *Comparisons*, to the *Ironist* for his *Sarcasmes:* to the *Apothegmatist* for his *Sentences*, &c., whereby a *Dedication* or *Speech* would be compos'd in a Moment, the superior Artist having nothing to do but to put together all the Materials.[4]

There are modern critics of Donne and his followers whose methods too often resemble those of Martinus Scriblerus.

In this preliminary chapter I have tried to show that the Augustans had a good deal in common with their predeces-

---

[1] It is also dangerous to try to identify a poet by his style in this period. Unless, indeed, there are examples of his work *in the same genre*, it is almost impossible. Pope—who had suffered from the habit—profoundly distrusted the use of stylistic 'evidence' of authorship (Spence, p. 168).

[2] See Dryden's remarks about Donne in the preface to *Eleonora* (1692).

[3] This is the subject of Rosemond Tuve's difficult but important book, *Elizabethan and Metaphysical Imagery* (1947).

[4] Ch. xiii.

sors of the late sixteenth and earlier seventeenth centuries. In poetry, as in politics and science, the seventeenth century was a period in which great changes were under way. It is not my object to minimize these changes. Nor should it be forgotten that the same body of critical theory supported work of very different sorts. Spenser, Milton, and Dryden all appealed to decorum, but they wrote very differently. Yet the fact that they could all appeal to decorum is of the greatest importance. To understand it is the first step to understanding their poetry. The remainder of this study is an examination of the ways in which the principle of decorum was interpreted in a number of poems by different writers. For this is a matter in which the empirical method is the only safe guide.

LOW SATIRE: *HUDIBRAS*

Nor is the world so well understood by observation of the little Good
that is in it, as the Prodigious variety of Wickednes Folly and
Madnes with which it is Possest.

BUTLER[1]

BUTLER took the name of his hero from Spenser, and his great comedy cannot be understood without glancing back to *The Faerie Queene*. In Book II, which is concerned with Temperaunce, Sir Guyon reaches a castle inhabited by three sisters. The youngest loves pleasure, the second moderation, while the third is a sour hater of all delights. Sir Hudibras, who is contrasted with Sans-loy, the wooer of the youngest sister, makes his suit to the eldest. In a stanza which throws a great deal of light on *Hudibras*, he is described as

> . . . an hardy man;
> Yet not so good of deedes, as great of name,
> Which he by many rash aduentures wan,
> Since errant armes to sew he first began;
> More huge in strength, then wise in workes he was,
> And reason with foole-hardize ouer ran;
> Sterne melancholy did his courage pas,
> And was for terrour more, all armd in shyning bras.[2]

'It is not unpleasant to observe', Butler once remarked, '. . . how all Sorts of men doe not only act but say things cleane Contrary to what they pretend and meane.'[3] For the reader who remembers his Spenser, this is the element of contradiction and inconsistency which the name Hudibras brings to mind. Butler's Hudibras resembles Spenser's in being more famous than he deserves, in having more strength than wisdom, and in being inspired less by true courage than by 'melancholy' (in this context, madness). But by giving his

---

[1] *Characters and Passages from Note-Books*, ed. A. R. Waller (1908), p. 344.
[2] II. ii, st. 17.   [3] *Characters*, p. 475.

hero this name Butler does not only indicate the main traits of his character: he also states his own attitude to the civil wars and the discontents which led up to them. The suggestion is that the Royalists, or the more extreme among them, bear an affinity to the youngest daughter Perissa and her lover Sans-loy; that the Parliamentary Party may be similarly compared to the eldest daughter and her wooer Hudibras; while the poet himself, and all moderate men, support the 'great rule of Temp'raunce'.[1]

The title is not the only thing about *Hudibras* which reminds one of *The Faerie Queene*. In its whole conception and organization Butler's poem has marked affinities with Spenser's. The parallel between the adventures of Sir Hudibras and those of the hero of each of the Books of *The Faerie Queene* must have been deliberate. Like one of Spenser's knights Butler's hero is involved in continual disputes and adventures, and woos a lady. But in all his endeavours he is an un-Spenserian failure.

The fact that Butler was familiar with the Renaissance doctrine of the heroic poem has a bearing on *Hudibras* which is frequently overlooked. Butler knew as well as Spenser or Milton that an allegorical meaning was expected in any long poem.

Betweene [error], and Truth [he wrote], ly's the Proper Sphere of wit, which though it seeme to incline to falshood, do's it only to give Intelligence[2] to Truth. . . . Wit by a certaine slight of the Minde, deliver's things otherwise then they are in Nature. . . . But when it imploys those things which it borrows of Falshood, to the Benefit and advantage of Truth, as in Allegories, Fables, and Apologues, it is of excellent use, as making a Deeper impression into the mindes of Men then if the same Truths were plainely deliver'd.[3]

Hudibras has something of the same complexity as *The Faerie Queene*. The strong element of the *roman à clef* has always been recognized; and there is no doubt that the poem was intended to embody a complicated allegory. As each of

---

[1] *The Faerie Queene*, ii, st. 5 of the Introduction, l. 9.
[2] intelligibility, expression.   [3] *Characters*, p. 336.

Spenser's knights represents one of the cardinal virtues, or the striving for that virtue, so Sir Hudibras represents one of the basic vices. Dennis suggested that *Hudibras* is a satire on hypocrisy:[1] Sir Hudibras is Hypocrisy embodied. Near the beginning of the poem the reader is told that 'Hipocrisie and Non-sence' are in control of Sir Hudibras's conscience;[2] hypocrisy is satirized with particular intensity throughout; and in the brilliant passage, parodying the confessional dialogues and self-communings of the Dissenters, in which Ralpho scares Hudibras into thinking him a supernatural 'Voice', he asks him point-blank:

> Why didst thou chuse that cursed Sin,
> Hypocrisie, to set up in?

To which the knight replies, without demur:

> Because it is the thriving'st Calling,
> The onely Saints-Bell that rings all in.[3]

Throughout *Hudibras* great emphasis is laid on the difference between profession and performance, outer seeming and inner reality.[4] It would hardly be an exaggeration to say that in this poem every species of human folly and crime is represented as a species of hypocrisy.

Although political satire is the most obvious 'end' of *Hudibras*, therefore, Hazlitt was right when he remarked that Butler 'could not, in spite of himself,

> narrow his mind
> And to party give up what was meant for mankind'.[5]

---

[1] See *The Characters and Conduct of Sir John Edgar, and his three Deputy-Governors* (1720), Letter III, in *The Critical Works of John Dennis*, ed. Edward Niles Hooker (1939, 1943), ii. 201.

[2] All quotations are from the 'Cambridge English Classics' text, ed. A. R. Waller (1905). Since the lines are not numbered in this edition, I give first the page-reference to it, and then in brackets the reference by part, canto, and line for users of other editions. This quotation is on p. 9 (I. i. 235).

[3] p. 228 (III. i. 1221–4).

[4] The word 'inward', which in such phrases as 'inward light' was a favourite with the Dissenters, occurs remarkably often in *Hudibras*, with satiric intention. It may not be an accident that Hudibras himself is first described to the reader serially, as it were: first his 'inside' and then his 'outward': p. 9 (I. i. 237–9). Cf. p. 131 (II. ii. 77–80).

[5] *Lectures on the English Comic Writers* ('World's Classics' edition, 1907), p. 78.

There are many passages where Butler makes no pretence
to be limiting his satire to a political party, but attacks
lawyers, women, the Royal Society, and pedantry of every
kind. If *Hudibras* had been completed it seems likely that
every type represented in Butler's prose 'Characters' would
have found its niche in a comprehensive 'Anatomy of
Melancholy'.

In giving his satire this wide scope Butler was following
the tradition of such works as Barclay's *Ship of Fools* and the
Encomium Moriae of Erasmus. Satire is like a shot fired at
sea: when it hits its target it causes a series of rings to radiate
outwards towards all other follies and vices whatever. And so
one finds in *Hudibras* strokes of general satire that have a
very wide application:

> . . . Most Men carry things so even
> Between this World, and Hell and Heaven,
> Without the least offence to either,
> They freely deal in all together.[1]

Butler had a great admiration for Ben Jonson,[2] and in some
respects he was his pupil. As in *Volpone* and *The Alchemist*
Jonson's main satire against greed is accompanied and enriched by incidental attacks on other species of folly and sin,
so in *Hudibras* hypocrisy is only the principal target. '[Butler]
in general ridicules not persons, but things', said Hazlitt,
'not a party, but their principles, which may belong, as time
and occasion serve, to one set of solemn pretenders or another.'[3] Because Butler was a man of genius what began
as a political burlesque ended as what Dennis truly called
a very just satire.[4]

---

[1] p. 203 (III. i. 213–16).

[2] See *Characters*, p. 399.

[3] p. 79. Cf. Butler's own remark: 'Wit is like Science not of Particulars, but universals,
for as Arguments drawn from Particulars signify little to universal Nature, which is the
Proper object of Science; so wit that is raysd upon any one Particular Person go's no further
unlesse it be from thence extended to all Human Nature.' *Characters*, p. 278.

[4] Hooker, ii. 201.

II

No passage in *Hudibras* is more familiar than that in which
Butler ridicules his hero's addiction to rhetoric:

> For *Rhetorick* he could not ope
> His mouth, but out there flew a Trope:
> And when he hapned to break off
> I'th'middle of his speech, or cough,
> H'had hard words, ready to shew why,
> And tell what Rules he did it by.[1]

Such satire was thoroughly conventional: one has only to
turn to Erasmus to find all the charges that Butler brings
against rhetorical pedantry brilliantly deployed by the
greatest of all the humanists.[2] What is satirized is not
rhetoric itself but the pedantic affectation of rhetoric, fine
words and elaborate figures out of season. It would be a
serious mistake to suppose that Butler is here rebelling
against old attitudes; and it would be equally false to imagine,
from his satire on rhetoric, that he himself had no use for it.
What Butler wrote of Sprat—'The Historian of Gresham
Colledge, Indevors to Cry down Oratory and Declamation,
while He uses nothing else'[3]—is equally true of himself.
The point is important because the modern reader, knowing
little of decorum and the kinds, has a natural tendency to
regard *Hudibras* as inspired doggerel and its author as a
literary jester who knew no other way of writing. Nothing
could be farther from the truth. Butler's other works make
it clear that Sir William Temple's description of Rabelais
as 'a Man of Excellent and Universal Learning as well as
Wit'[4] is no less applicable to him.

It follows that Butler's choice of verse and style was
perfectly deliberate. The limited value of metrical notations
appears in the fact that the same name must be given to the
metre of *Hudibras* as to that of Marvell's *To his Coy Mistress*

---

[1] p. 5 (I. i. 81–86).

[2] See *Moriæ Encomium: or A Panegyrick upon Folly . . . Done into English* (1709), pp. 6–7,
117–23, *et ubique*.

[3] *Characters*, p. 424.   [4] 'Of Poetry', in Spingarn, iii. 101.

and *The Garden*, as well as many parts of *L'Allegro* and *Il Penseroso*. Like the iambic pentameter, the tetrameter is endlessly adaptable: it is the use that Butler makes of it, the tune that he plays on it, that is significant. His verse 'stands indeed upon Four Feet', as an anonymous critic remarked in 1698;

> but its Liberties and Priveleges are unbounded; and those Four Feet are, I think, by no means oblig'd to be but Eight Syllables; for in place of the Last, it is a part of its Excellency sometimes to have Two, Three, or Four Syllables (like so many Claws) crowded into the Time of One Foot. . . . It is wonderful to traverse its Arbitrary Power, how it proceeds without regard to *Periods*, *Colons*, or *Comma*'s: How sometimes it will change *Accents* for the sake of *Rhyme*, and, according to the most vulgar and careless Pronunciation, leave out what *Consonants* it pleases. . . .[1]

What is particularly remarkable is the rushing vigour of *Hudibras*, the unfailing energy of the verse.

In reflective and sententious passages, which are among the most brilliant parts of the poem, Butler often confines the sense to couplets for twenty or thirty lines at a time. On such occasions the affinity of his verse to familiar proverbs is particularly evident. But the 'numbers' of the poem, as Johnson pointed out, are 'purposely neglected'.[2] There are examples enough to show that 'harmonious verse' was well within Butler's reach; but he seldom wanted it. Instead there are frequent harsh enjambements.[3]

The effect of these enjambements is often enhanced by the rhymes. Rhyme fulfils different functions in the hands of different poets. In Pope, very often, it perfects the epigram: in Tennyson it serves most characteristically as an addition to the orchestral resources: in Butler, as Dennis understood, it is frequently part of the satire. 'A Rime alone

---

[1] The Advertisement to *Pendragon; or, the Carpet Knight His Kalender* (1698), an anonymous burlesque poem, pp. [A2ᵛ–A3ᵛ]. Quoted by Bond, *English Burlesque Poetry, 1700–1750* (1932), pp. 34–35.

[2] *Lives of the English Poets*, ed. G. B. Hill (1905), i. 217.

[3] Cf. the 'harshness' expected of satire in the late sixteenth and early seventeenth centuries.

is very often a Jest', he remarked, 'as all who are acquainted with *Hudibras* very well know.'[1] For example,

> He us'd to lay about and stickle,
> Like *Ram* or *Bull*, at *Conventicle*;[2]

or again:

> Madam, *I do, as is my Duty,*
> *Honour the Shadow of your Shoe-tye.*[3]

Perhaps the odd rhymes have too often distracted attention from the more solid wit of *Hudibras*, as Addison thought.[4] They are certainly less numerous than is commonly supposed.

'Il est vif & serré, & dit en peu de vers, ce qu'ils [his imitators] étendroient en une longue Kirielle de rimes.'[5] This praise of Scarron may be allowed to draw attention to one of the sovereign merits of Butler's use of the tetrameter, his power of gaining effects of remarkable brevity. Sometimes he takes pleasure in spinning out a far-fetched thought; but when he wants to be concise he cuts language to the bone.

The question of Butler's forerunners and models is not very important. Some such use of the tetrameter as his must always have been common in lampoons and other popular sorts of verse, such as the vulgar ballad. It may be found here and there in the Middle Ages, as in the satirical parts of *Le Roman de la Rose*. Scarron, with whose work Butler's shares 'une trompeuse facilité',[6] must have been familiar to him; and he may well have taken a hint from the authors of certain of the poems in *Musarum Deliciæ* and *Wit Restor'd*, two witty miscellanies published in 1656 and 1658.[7] But no earlier poet of genius had specialized in the satirical use of this metre.

---

1 Preface to *Britannia Triumphans* (1704). Hooker, i. 377.   2 p. 39 (I. ii. 437–8).

3 p. 201 (III. i. 163–4).   For the rhyme cf. Crashaw's *Wishes To his (supposed) Mistresse*, ll. 17–18.   4 The *Spectator*, No. 249.

5 'Discours sur le Style Burlesque en general, et sur celui de Mr. Scarron en particulier', prefixed to *Œuvres de Monsieur Scarron, Nouvelle Edition* (1737), 10 vols., vol. i. 137.

6 Ibid., p. 118.

7 See, too, a number of the pieces assembled in *Rump: or an Exact Collection Of the Choycest Poems and Songs Relating to the Late Times. By the most Eminent Wits, from Anno 1639 to Anno 1661* (1662): particularly those on pp. 35, 50, 68, 85, and 209 of vol. i of the 1874 reprint.

Butler's metre cannot usefully be considered in isolation from the other aspects of his idiom, for there is a perfect partnership between his versification and his diction. Even if the verse itself were what is misleadingly termed 'heroic' (iambic pentameters rhyming in pairs), any serious attempt at the 'harmonious numbers' appropriate to heroic verse in the full sense would be ludicrously out of place as an accompaniment to the prosaic diction which is Butler's chosen medium.[1] For this reason Dryden's censure of the metre of *Hudibras*[2] must be read rather as a reflection of his own choice of a suitable metre for satire than as impartial literary criticism.

As is natural in a poem of such length—there is a greater number of lines in *Hudibras* than in *Paradise Lost*—the style varies considerably from passage to passage; but the staple of the idiom is a personal development of the least elevated of the three styles distinguished by Renaissance and Augustan rhetoricians, the 'low' style appropriate to the base sort of satire. Occasionally, indeed, Butler satirizes by describing his butts sarcastically in elevated language:

> 'Mong these the fierce *Magnano* was,
> And *Talgol* foe to *Hudibras*;
> *Cerdon* and *Colon*, Warriors stout
> And resolute as ever fought:
> Whom furious *Orsin* thus bespoke.[3]

And sometimes Butler reminds the reader of Dryden's description of *La Secchia Rapita*, alternating with lines which seem 'majestical and severe' afterthoughts which 'turn them all into a pleasant ridicule':[4]

> Next march'd brave *Orsin*, famous for
> Wise Conduct, and success in War:
> A skilful Leader, stout, severe,
> *Now Marshal to the Champion Bear.*

[1] A point made by Dennis (Preface to *Miscellanies in Verse and Prose* (1693), in Hooker, i. 8), and by Johnson (*Lives*, i. 217). On 'heroic verse' cf. p. 60, n. 1, below.
[2] *Essays*, ii. 105–6. Quoted in part on p. 44.
[3] p. 65 (i. iii. 243–7).
[4] *Essays*, ii. 107.

> With Truncheon tip'd with Iron head,
> The Warrior to the Lists [he] led;
> With solemn march and stately pace,
> *But far more grave and solemn face.*[1]

But although tetrameters were occasionally used with a heroic idiom, the metre of *Hudibras* is not well suited to ironical solemnity. The sustained irony of the mock-heroic was not Butler's goal. Whenever he essays it, one senses his natural bent to downright ridicule impatiently waiting for its chance.

The characteristic mode of satire in *Hudibras* is the opposite of the mock-heroic, that of describing everything in the most undignified manner possible:

> When civil fury first grew high,
> And men *fell out* they knew not why,
> When hard Words, Jealousies, and Fears, .
> *Set* Folks together *by the Ears*,
> And made them *fight*, *like mad or drunk*,
> For *Dame* Religion *as for Punk*,
> Whose honesty they all durst *swear for*,
> Though *not a man of them knew wherefore.*[2]

Satire and the sympathetic feelings are absolutely incompatible. Butler's object in these lines, the essential satirist's object, is to kill any sympathy which the reader may feel for the subject of his satire, moving him instead to amusement and contempt. Nor is there anything indirect in the working of the satire. The method is that of straightforward 'diminution': the reader is told that the quarrels which led to the civil war were of no more account than a brawl for a whore, and his acceptance of this view is made inevitable (at least temporarily) by the fact that the whole affair is described in an idiom which ridicules everything it touches.[3] Butler's subject is as different as possible from that of the romantic epic poet. Instead of Ariosto's

---

[1] p. 32 (I. ii. 147–54). My italics.

[2] p. 3 (I. i. 1–8). I have italicized the 'lowest' words and turns of phrase, and ignored the italics in the text. It would be interesting to know why Butler rejected 'civil Dudgeon', the reading of the first edition.

[3] It is interesting to compare the opening of *Hudibras* with that of an attempt at serious heroic verse in the same metre, Sir Arthur Gorges's translation of Lucan's *Pharsalia* (1614):

> Le donne, i cavallier, l'arme, gli amori,
> Le cortesie, l'audaci imprese,

he is concerned with light wenches and prudish viragos, costermongers and fanatics, rudeness in every sense and of every kind. And his style is equally remote from that of heroic verse. The elementary principle on which he works is that while many people might sympathize with a *crowd*, no one cares to take sides with a *rout*. The essence of low satire could not be more simple.

The nature of Butler's low style is nowhere more evident than in the *sententiae*. Following the rhetorical precept of the time, Butler made considerable use of this figure, particularly at such points as the beginning and end of a canto;[1] but while sententious passages are often written in a high style, those in *Hudibras* are in the most colloquial language:

> Ay me! what perils do environ
> The Man that meddles with cold Iron!
> What plaguy mischiefs and mishaps
> Do dog him still with after-claps!
> For though Dame Fortune seem to smile
> And leer upon him for a while;
> She'll after shew him, in the nick
> Of all his Glories, a Dog-trick.[2]

> A More then ciuill warre I sing,
> That through th' *Emathian* fields did ring,
> Where reins let loose to head-strong pride,
> A potent people did misguide:
> Whose conquering hand enrag'd rebounds
> On his owne bowels with deepe wounds.
> Where Hosts confronting neare alies,
> All faith and Empires Lawes defies.
> A world of force in faction meetes,
> And common guilt like torrents fleets.
> Where like infestuous ensignes waue, ⎫
> The *Ægle* doth the *Ægle* braue,   ⎬
> And *Pyle* against the *Pyle* doth raue. ⎭

This is indifferent heroic verse, and Butler parodied a passage from the same poem (p. 41 (I. ii. 493 et seq.)); but there is a pronounced difference of diction between the heroic passage and the low satirical one.

[1] e.g. p. 58 (I. ii. 1177-8); p. 129 (II. ii. 1-24); p. 152 (II. iii. 1-36); pp. 197-8 (III. i. 1-30); pp. 283-4 (III. iii. 1-32).

[2] p. 59 (I. iii. 1-8).

The contrast between these lines and the opening couplet of *MacFlecknoe*, which is equally sententious, affords a vivid example of the difference between the low style and the heroic:

> All humane things are subject to decay,
> And, when Fate summons, Monarchs must obey.[1]

While it could hardly be more different in style, *Hudibras* like *MacFlecknoe* belongs to the class of satires which Dryden named Varronian. The basis of the poem is narrative. To call it a 'burlesque' is to invite confusion. If the essence of burlesque consists in describing dignified characters and actions (which are usually not of the poet's invention) in a ludicrous manner, then the parts of *Hudibras* which deal directly with the wars may be so described. But the poem as a whole is the result of an act of the creative imagination. Only in the sense that the whole world of *Hudibras* symbolizes the civil wars can its heart be said to consist in a discrepancy between subject and style. Sir Hudibras and the adventures he meets with as he rides 'a Colonelling' are extremely undignified. When they are described in a low style the result is not incongruity but rather a perfect aptness: the style matches the characters and action. The result is that it can only be misleading to compare *Hudibras* with such burlesques as Cotton's *Virgil Travestie*.

III

All has not been said of the 'original and peculiar'[2] diction of *Hudibras* when it has been assigned to the category of low style. It is remarkably varied. The second paragraph of

---

[1] Although 'low' words are Butler's staple, it is possible to distinguished a peculiar sort of prosaisms which he also employs—phrases such as 'Before we f[ur]ther do proceed, It doth behove us to say something', p. 14 (I. i. 420–1); 'Assist me but this once, I'mplore, And I shall trouble thee no more' p. 20 (I. i. 663–4); or 'This *Ralpho* knew, and therefore took The other course, of which we spoke', p. 19 (I. i. 621–2). Such words are not precisely 'low'; but they have a 'non-conducting' quality which makes them fatal to poetry of an elevated sort. Butler uses them for bathos, and to parody the flat phraseology of many of the Dissenters.

[2] Johnson, *Lives*, i. 209.

the poem, for example, introduces a new element, that of parody:

> A *Wight* he was, whose very sight wou'd
> Entitle him *Mirror of Knighthood*;
> That never bent *his stubborn knee*
> To any thing but *Chivalry*.[1]

This element of literary satire demands modifications of style which enhance the variety of the poem.

The critical attitude which inspires the parodies in *Hudibras* is precisely that which one would expect of Butler, an Augustan conservatism looking back to classical models and suspicious of innovation. The principal targets are such writers of 'romantic' epics as Ariosto, Spenser, and Davenant. Other unclassical genres which are parodied include the ballad,[2] the metrical romance of the Middle Ages, which survived among humble readers during the seventeenth century, and the prose heroic romances so popular in France and England during Butler's lifetime. Although Butler has his fling at modern translators, the great classical epics themselves are parodied comparatively seldom.[3]

The literary satire which finds expression in perpetual 'allusions' thoughout *Hudibras* is only one aspect of a comprehensive critique of the uses and abuses of the English language. No less than Rabelais or James Joyce, Butler was a fascinated student of language. Odd words interested him as much as odd ideas. It would not be hard to imagine him spending an evening with Robert Burton listening to the swearing of the bargees at Folly Bridge. It may be that he had no need to go out of his way to find freaks of language. If there is any truth in the tradition that he was at one time secretary to Sir Samuel Luke, he must have had every opportunity of hearing the latest in cant terms. Perhaps he used some of his numerous notebooks[4] for recording the

---

[1] p. 4 (I. i. 15-18). My italics.   [2] *Chevy Chace* is parodied at p. 62 (I. iii. 95-96).

[3] A shift in the primary meaning of the word 'burlesque' has led many modern readers to exaggerate the importance of the parodic element in *Hudibras*. The main aim of the poem is not parody but satire.

[4] Butler's reliance on notebooks is one of many traits reminiscent of Bacon. But the habit was, of course, widespread.

words he heard. With an intense satiric mastery he culled
the language of sectarians and pedants of every sort. *Hudibras* became the receptacle of this wealth of strange words;
as a result it has a greater variety of idiom than any other
poem in the language.

Yet it would be quite wrong to think of Butler simply as
an enthusiast for 'stunning words'—however different his
criterion from Rossetti's.[1] He lived in an age of linguistic
flux when the native genius of 'the finest of the vernacular
tongues' seemed to many good judges to be in peril. Sprat
complained that the language had 'receiv'd many fantastical
terms, which were introduced by our *Religious Sects* . . .
and *Translators*'.[2] Dryden returned to this subject time and
time again. 'I have endeavoured to write English', he wrote
in his first considerable critical essay, which appeared in the
same year as the Second Part of *Hudibras*, 'as near as I
could distinguish it from the tongue of pedants, and that of
affected travellers. Only I am sorry, that (speaking so noble
a language as we do) we have not a more certain measure of
it, as they have in France'.[3] In this revival of the Renaissance
zeal for ennobling the vernacular Butler played his own part.
'That Barbarous Canting which those use who do not understand the sense and Propriety of a Language'[4] is continually
a target of his satire.

All the abilities of our moderne Guifted men consist in fantastique
Senseles expressions, and silly affected Phrases [he complained in one
of his notebooks] just in such a Stile as the great Turke, and the
Persian Sophy use to write, which they believe to be the true Propriety
of the Spirit, and highest perfection of all Sanctity . . . Like a Spell or
charme, [Cant] has a wonderful operation [on] the Rabble, for they
Naturally admire any unusuall words which they do not understand,
but would gladly seeme to do, as believing all wisdome as these men do
all holines to consist in words.[5] They call their Gifts Dispensations,

---

[1] 'I have been reading up all manner of old romaunts, to pitch upon stunning words for
poetry.' (*Dante Gabriel Rossetti: His Family Letters* (1895), ii. 51.)

[2] *History of the Royal-Society*, p. 42.

[3] *Epistle Dedicatory of the Rival Ladies* (1664), in *Essays*, i. 5.

[4] *Characters*, p. 467.

[5] Remarks as commonplace as this are sometimes quoted as examples of the rebellion against

because they believe God do's dispence with them for any wickednes which [they] can Commit.[1]

'This Canting runs through all Professions and Sorts of men', Butler added, 'from the Judge on the Bench to the Begger in the Stocks'; and he laid all these sources under contribution for his great satire. Sidrophel, with his lore of Paracelsus, 'Behmen' and 'the dog of Cacodemon', has at his tongue's end all the cant of his kind:

> Quoth *Whachum*, *Venus* you retriv'd,
> In opposition with *Mars*,
> And no benigne friendly Stars
> T'allay th'effect. Quoth *Wizard*, So!
> In *Virgo*? Ha! quoth *Whachum*, No.
> Has *Saturn* nothing to do in't?
> One tenth of's *Circle* to a minute.[2]

Butler's use of the special vocabularies of trades and professions may be regarded as a satirical footnote to the dispute about 'terms of art' which raged so fiercely from the early Renaissance onwards. 'The Tearms of all Arts are generally Nonsense', he wrote, 'that signify nothing, or very improperly what they are Meant to do, and are more Difficult to be learn'd then the things they are designd to teach.'[3] The cant of lawyers he found even more objectionable than that of astrologers; it is satirized in the language of the practitioner whom Sir Hudibras consults about his complicated affairs. He says that he can find his client plenty of 'Knights of the Post', ne'er-do-wells who live

> [By] letting out to hire, their Ears,
> To Affidavit-Customers:
> At inconsiderable values,
> To serve for Jury-men, or Tales,[4]

rhetoric which is supposed to be characteristic of 'The Age of the Royal Society'. Butler, like Sprat, sees that knowledge does not consist merely in words. Erasmus and Pope would have agreed; indeed who would not? Such a passage should act as a safeguard against facile generalizations. For Butler was no rebel: he was a thoroughly traditional humanist.

[1] *Characters*, p. 312.   [2] p. 165 (II. iii. 530–6).
[3] *Characters*, p. 445.   [4] 'Tales' is a legal term.

> Although retain'd in th' hardest matters,
> Of Trustees, and Administrators.[1]

The affectation of legal terms by the half-educated so common among the Roundheads is unsparingly parodied in the
speeches of Sir Hudibras, who delights to give authority
to his pronouncements by a judicious smattering of the 'Barbarous French'[2] and Latin of the law:

> And therefore being inform'd by bruit,
> That *Dog* and *Bear* are to dispute;
> For so of.late men fighting name,
> Because they often prove the same;
> (For where the first does hap to be
> The last does *coincidere*)
> *Quantum in nobis*, have thought good,
> To save th'expence of Christian blood,
> And try if we by Mediation
> Of Treaty and accomodation
> Can end the quarrel.[3]

Sir Hudibras's verbal habits are precisely those which John
Eachard censured when he described 'a sort of Divines, who,
if they but happen of an unlucky hard word all the week, . . .
think themselves not careful of their flock, if they lay it not
up till Sunday, and bestow it amongst them, in their next
preachment'.[4] Like Eachard's preacher, the Knight disdains
words 'such as the constable uses' as much as matter 'such
as comes to the common market'.

Another form of pedantry common among the Dissenters
and parodied in *Hudibras* is the affected use of terms from
formal logic. 'It would be possible', said Hazlitt, 'to deduce
the different forms of syllogism in Aristotle, from the different violations or mock imitations of them in Butler.'[5]
Such passages show that in Butler parody of a man's idiom is

---

[1] p. 302 (III. iii. 729–34).

[2] *Characters*, p. 445.

[3] p. 22 (I. i. 721–31).

[4] *The Grounds, & Occasions of the Contempt of the Clergy and Religion Enquired into*, in
Arber's *English Garner*, vii (1883), p. 268.

[5] *Lectures on the English Comic Writers*, p. 79.

inseparable from satire on the cast of his mind.[1] He particularly rejoices in 'metaphysical' arguments which prove
that black is white or deal in matters completely unrelated
to the realities of life:

> The Question then, to state it first,
> Is which is *better*, or which *worst*,
> *Synods* or *Bears*?[2]

A choice example of this sort of dialectic parodies the species
of elegant sophistry of which Lovelace's *To Althea from Prison*
is the best-known example:

> . . . Th'one half of Man, his Mind
> Is *Sui juris* unconfin'd,
> And cannot be laid by the heels,
> What e'er the other moiety feels.
> 'Tis not Restraint or Liberty
> That makes Men prisoners or free;
> But perturbations that possess
> The Mind or Æquanimities.[3]

Equally masterly is Butler's exposition of the problem of
pain.[4] In such passages he directs against the sects precisely
the charges which Reformation satirists had so frequently
hurled against the Catholic Church. The Lady explicitly
compares Sir Hudibras's skill in argument with that of the
most subtle of the Catholic orders :

> You have provided well, *quoth She*,
> (I thank you) for your self and me;
> And shewn your *Presbyterian* wits
> Jump punctual with the *Jesuits*.[5]

IV

While the diction of *Hudibras* is remarkably varied, it is
the astonishing profusion of witty images that distinguishes

[1] See, for example, the reflections of Sir Hudibras and his humble confession, when what
he took for 'some drolling Sprite' relates the story of his sins : pp. 231 et seq. (III. i. 1339 et
seq.).   [2] p. 92 (I. iii. 1265-7).
[3] p. 85 (I. iii. 1013-20).
[4] p. 110 (II. i. 183 et seq.).
[5] p. 210 (III. i. 497-500).

it most sharply from the common run of burlesques. It is
clear from the 'character' of *A Small Poet* and from numerous
prose jottings that Butler was keenly interested in the ana-
logical uses of language. Like Bacon's, indeed, his was 'a
mind keenly sensitive to all analogies and affinities . . .
spreading as it were tentacles on all sides in quest of chance
prey'.[1] If ever a man was haunted by 'the demon of analogy',
it was he.

As one would expect, a very large number of the images in
Hudibras are of the 'diminishing' sort characteristic of direct
satire. Fat bawds are

> All Guts and Belly like a Crab.[2]

Clever people

> . . . [keep] their *Consciences* in Cases,
> As *Fidlers* do their *Crowds*[3] and *Bases*,
> Ne'er to be us'd but when they're bent
> To play a fit for *Argument*.[4]

'Many Heads'

> obstruct Intrigues,
> As slowest Insects have most Legs.[5]

The realistic bent of Butler's mind led him to fill his satire
with imagery from the most commonplace objects of daily
use, 'Out-of-fashion'd Cloaths', bowls, watches that go
'sometime too fast, sometime too slow', 'a Candle in the
Socket', and beer 'by Thunder turn'd to Vineger'.[6] He takes
his choice from the familiar things of the farmyard and
kitchen-hearth, children's games and men's employments.
Images from animals are particularly common. Mahomet

> Had Lights where better Eyes were blind,
> As Pigs are said to see the Wind.[7]

---

[1] R. W. Church, *Bacon* ('English Men of Letters' series, ed. of 1884), p. 24.
[2] p. 261 (III. ii. 874).   [3] 'A fiddle' (Johnson).
[4] p. 129 (II. ii. 5–8).   [5] p. 246 (III. ii. 265–6).
[6] p. 272 (III. ii. 1298); p. 269 (III. ii. 1156); p. 276 (III. ii. 1464); p. 224 (III. i. 1051);
p. 31 (I. ii. 110).
[7] p. 267 (III. ii. 1107–8).

The Rump Parliament

>   With new Reversions of nine Lives,
>   Starts up, and, like a Cat, revives.[1]

We Dissenters—says one of them—have friends who

>   Are only Tools to our Intrigues,
>   And sit like Geese to hatch our Eggs.[2]

Again,

>   . . . All Religions flock together,
>   Like Tame, and Wild-Fowl of a Feather.[3]

These are only a few of the animal-images from a single canto:[4] to quote more would be tedious. What is remarkable is the effect that Butler achieves. By crowding his poem with similes from animals of 'low' associations like dogs, cats, pigs, and mice ('Valor's a Mouse-trap, Wit a Gin, Which Women oft are taken in'[5]) he gains an effect of homely caricature. The reader feels that no more is needed to demonstrate the folly of Butler's targets than reference to the store of common sense summed up in the nation's proverbs and homely sayings.

In a poem as long as *Hudibras* it is natural that a poet with a passion for images should have drawn on many aspects of life for his analogies. It is unnecessary to give examples of similes from law, low life, politics, religion, and the rest: they may be found on every page. The prevalent tone, however, remains that given by the 'low' comparisons which are so numerous. This is not least clear when Butler is dealing with abstractions:

>   He'd extract numbers out of matter,
>   And keep them in a Glass, like water.
>
>   .   .   .   .
>
>   By help of these (as he profest)
>   He had *First Matter* seen undrest:

---

[1] p. 281 (III. ii. 1629–30).
[2] p. 262 (III. ii. 895–6).
[3] p. 276 (III. ii. 1455–6).
[4] The second canto of the Third Part is much the richest in imagery.
[5] p. 69 (I. iii. 391–2).

> He took her naked all alone,
> Before one Rag of *Form* was on.[1]

Or again:

> Honour is, like a Widow, won
> With brisk Attempt and putting on;
> With ent'ring manfully, and urging;
> Not slow approaches, like a Virgin.[2]

Butler was remarkably skilled in this art of finding a concrete image for an abstract idea. Such images parody one of the commonest habits of the Dissenting preachers, many of whom had a passion for the more abstruse reaches of theology for which they were ill fitted by education.

Decorum and common sense alike required that there should be more images in some parts of the poem than in others. 'The Nature of a Narrative', Butler noted, 'require's nothing but a Plaine, and Methodicall Accompt of Matter of Fact Without Reflictions, and witty observations on the by, which are more Proper for Discourses, and Repartees.'[3] That is not true of the kind of satirical narrative that one finds in *Hudibras*. Yet it is very noticeable that the speeches contain far more metaphors and similes than the rest of the poem; it is because the speeches together make up a large part of the whole that Butler was able to indulge so fully his passion for fantastic figures.

In creating this profusion of imagery Butler was again adapting to the purposes of his own satire a common practice of the Dissenters, who were accused, with justice, of being 'indiscreet and horrid Metaphor-mongers'. 'As for the common sort of people that are addicted to this sort of expression in their discourses', Eachard complained in 1670, 'away presently to both the Indies! rake heaven and earth! down to the bottom of the sea! then tumble over all Arts and Sciences! ransack all shops and warehouses! spare neither camp nor city, but that they will have them!'[4] Sir

---

[1] pp. 17–18 (i. i. 553–4 and 559–62).   [2] pp. 26–27 (i. i. 911–14).
[3] *Characters*, p. 466.   [4] Eachard, in Arber, vii, p. 272.

Hudibras's proud principle, never to speak 'to Man or Beast, In notions vulgarly exprest',[1] inspires the speeches of many of Butler's characters: in nothing is its meaning more clearly illustrated than in their imagery:

> For, as in Bodies Natural,
> The Rump's the Fundament of all;
> So, in a Commonwealth, or Realm,
> The Government is call'd the Helm:
> With which, like Vessels under Sail,
> Th'are turn'd and winded by the Tail.
> The Tail, which Birds and Fishes steer
> Their Courses with, through Sea and Air;
> To whom the Rudder of the Rump is
> The same thing With the Stern and Compass.
> This shews, how perfectly the Rump
> And Commonwealth in Nature jump.
> For, as a Fly, that goes to Bed,
> Rests with his Tail above his Head;
> So in this Mungril State of ours,
> The Rabble are the Supreme Powers.
> That Hors'd us on their Backs to show us
> A Jadish trick at last, and throw us.[2]

Again:

> For as the *Persian Magi* once
> Upon their *Mothers* got their *Sons*,
> Who were incapable t'injoy
> That Empire any other way:
> So *Presbyter* begot the other
> Upon the *Good Old Cause*, his Mother,
> That bore them like the Devil's Dam,
> Whose *Son* and *Husband* are the same.[3]

As might be expected, it is not only the Dissenters whose verbal habits are parodied in the imagery of *Hudibras*. A connoisseur of folly in all its forms, Butler was equally amused by the extravagances of the poets of his day, and satirized their commonplace images:

[1] p. 109 (II. i. 157–8).   [2] p. 280 (III. ii. 1597–1614).
[3] pp. 239–40 (III. ii. 13–20).

> Some with *Arabian Spices* strive
> To embalm her cruelly alive;
> Or *season* her, as *French* Cooks use
> Their *Haut-gusts, Buollies,* or *Ragusts;*
> Use her so barbarously ill,
> To grind her Lips upon a *Mill,*
> Until the *Facet Doublet* doth
> Fit their *Rhimes* rather than her mouth;
> Her mouth compar'd t' an *Oyster's,* with
> A row of *Pearl* in't, stead of *Teeth.*[1]

Of the prevalent fashions none interested Butler more than the different varieties of the Metaphysical idiom, now (in spite of numerous late appearances) past its heyday. As he turned the pages of such poets as Donne and Cowley and his friends Davenant and Cleveland[2] there was nothing that drew his attention more frequently than their bold juxtapositions of ideas. His own relation to the Metaphysical poets is never more evident than in some of his images:

> His Body, that stupendious Frame,
> Of all the World the Anagram,
> Is of two equal parts compact
> In Shape and Symmetry exact.
> Of which the Left and Female side
> Is to the Manly Right a Bride.[3]

The satirical tendency implicit in Metaphysical poetry from the first is very marked in the work of Cleveland; in Butler, it might be said, this tendency becomes fully developed. The truth is rather that Butler was the first comic poet to invade the territory of Metaphysical verse and use with

---

[1] p. 120 (II. i. 595–604). Such complaints are no doubt as old as love-poetry itself. Cf., for example, Shakespeare's *Sonnets,* cxxx.

[2] Butler and Cleveland seem to have been close friends. Aubrey tells us that they 'had a clubb every night' (*Brief Lives,* ed. Clark (1898), i. 175). Mr. J. T. Curtiss's conjecture that 'some of *Hudibras* was set down at these meetings' is an attractive one (*P.M.L.A.,* Dec. 1929). Wit flourishes at such meetings—witness the Scriblerus Club fifty years later.

Farmer amused himself by marking in his copy of Cleveland the passages from which Butler had taken hints for *Hudibras.* (See Bishop Percy, in *Biographia Britannica,* iii. 632 n.; quoted by A. H. Nethercot in 'The Reputation of the "Metaphysical Poets" during the Age of Johnson and the "Romantic Revival"' (*S.P.* Jan. 1925, p. 111 n.).)

[3] p. 217 (III. i. 771–6).

genius the spoils that he found there. More brilliantly than any previous poet, he used 'wit' for the purposes of low satire. As a result he occupies a distinctive place in the evolution of the idioms of English poetry in the later seventeenth century. *Hudibras* was one of the principal channels by which the 'wit' of the earlier part of the century was transmitted to the greatest of the Augustans.[1]

Yet it would be a mistake to think of Butler too narrowly as a satirist. Dennis found 'a vivacity and purity in his Language, *whereever it was fit it should be pure*, that could proceed from nothing but from a generous Education, and from a happy Nature'.[2] Such a passage as this illustrates what Dennis meant:

> For though out-number'd, overthrown,
> And by the Fate of War run down;
> Their Duty never was defeated,
> Nor from their Oaths and Faith retreated.
> *For Loyalty is still the same,*
> *Whether it win or lose the Game;*
> *True as a Dial to the Sun,*
> *Although it be not shin'd upon.*[3]

This is not 'high style', which would be out of place; but there are no cant terms in these lines, the diction is pure, and the image is handled with a remarkable felicity. The same is true of the *Heroical Epistle of Hudibras to his Lady*, which is not the work of a man completely unskilled in the mode of writing which it parodies. The man who could write like this:

> The *Sun* grew low, and left the Skies,
> Put down (some write) by *Ladies* eyes.
> The *Moon* pull'd off her veil of Light,
> That hides her face by day from sight,
> (Mysterious Veil, of brightness made,
> That's both her lustre, and her shade).[4]

---

[1] Voltaire said that it was the wittiest poem that he had ever read: *Lettres Philosophiques*, xxii. a.i.

[2] Preface to *Miscellanies in Verse and Prose* (1693), in Hooker, i. 7. (My italics.)

[3] pp. 243–4 (III. ii. 169–76).   [4] p. 128 (II. i. 903–8).

was no *mere* burlesque-writer. And indeed *Hudibras* contains
a number of passages that would lend distinction to any
lyric of the age:

> For as we see th'eclipsed Sun
> By mortals is more gaz'd upon,
> Than when adorn'd with all his light
> He shines in Serene Sky most bright:
> So Valor in a low estate
> Is most admir'd and wonder'd at.[1]

No 'Caroline lyrist' could do better than this:

> To bid me not to *love*,
> Is to forbid my *Pulse* to move,[2]

or excel this image, perhaps the finest of all:

> Like *Indian*-Widows, gone to Bed
> In Flaming Curtains to the Dead.[3]

Such a simile reminds one for a moment that Butler was a
younger contemporary of Henry King. Occasionally in reading him one hears the rhythms of the Caroline lyric resonant
beneath the surface of the verse. A gift for epigram was not
the only thing he had in common with Andrew Marvell.[4]

In spite of the 'kinds' there was in the seventeenth century
no such hard and fast distinction between 'poetry' (conceived of as a serious and indeed solemn thing) and 'light
verse' as became a commonplace in the nineteenth century.
As many of the love poems of the time make clear, verse was

---

[1] p. 86 (I. iii. 1051–6).   [2] p. 114 (II. i. 343–4).
[3] p. 213 (III. i. 639–40).

[4] I am thinking particularly of the Marvell of the *Horatian Ode*. Conversely, as Mr.
Geoffrey Walton has pointed out in 'The Poetry of Andrew Marvell: A Summing Up'
(*Politics and Letters*, No. 4, Summer 1948), Marvell has at times a 'Hudibrastic jocularity'.
It would not be easy to say which of the two following quotations was from Butler:

> (i) But their lowd'st Cannon were their Lungs;
> And sharpest Weapons were their tongues.
> (ii) The Conjugal Petard, that tears
> Down all Portcullices of Ears,
> And makes the Volly of one Tongue
> For all their Leathern Shields too strong.

The first is from *Upon Appleton House*, pp. 255–6, the second from *Hudibras*, p. 216 (III. i.
745–8). Marvell thought highly of Butler's satire, although it was directed against his own
party; see *The Rehearsal Transpros'd: The Second Part* (1674), p. 334.

a much subtler instrument then than it was later to become. A poet could modulate from one level of seriousness to another in a couplet, or within a single line. Satire and elegy, burlesque and 'the lyric note' were not always mutually exclusive. The best Augustan poetry retains something of this subtlety of tone.

V

When *Hudibras* is regarded simply as a long satiric or comic poem Butler's mastery in many of the traditional branches of the poet's art becomes evident. Since he commonly receives less than his due and has been the subject of remarkably little criticism of late, I wish to conclude this chapter with some examples of his skill.

Many passages from the speeches which are among the most remarkable features of the poem have already been quoted. One more must suffice. It is made by a messenger who rushes up to Hudibras and his friends 'pale as Death', to gasp out his story 'by fits':

> That beastly Rabble,—that came down
> From all the Garrets—in the Town,
> And Stalls, and Shop-boards,—in vast Swarms,
> With new-chalk'd Bills,—and rusty Arms,
> To cry the Cause—up, heretofore,
> And bawl the Bishops—out of Door;
> Are now drawn up,—in greater Shoals,
> To Roast—and Boil us on the Coals:
> And all the Grandees—of our Members
> Are Carbonading on—the Embers;
> Knights, Citizens and Burgesses—
> Held forth by Rumps—of Pigs and Geese.
> That serve for Characters—and Badges,
> To represent their Personages.[1]

Examples of Butler's skill as a narrative and descriptive poet are equally numerous:

[1] p. 278 (III. ii. 1505 et seq.).

And now the cause of all their *fear*,
By slow degrees approach'd so near,
They might distinguish diff'rent noise
Of *Horns*, and *Pans*, and *Dogs*, and *Boys*,
And *Kettle Drums*, whose sullen *Dub*
Sounds like the hooping of a *Tub*:
But when the Sight appear'd in view,
They found it was an antique Show:

.   .   .

And follow'd with a world of *Tall* Lads,
That merry *Ditties* trol'd, and *Ballads*;
Did ride, with many a good morrow,
Crying, *hey for our Town* through the *Burrough*.[1]

No English poet has written with more zest than Butler,
or more vividly:

When *Tinkers* bawl'd aloud, to settle
Church Discipline, for patching *Kettle*.
No *Sow-gelder* did blow his Horn
To geld a Cat, but cry'd *Reform*.
The *Oyster-wom[e]n* lock'd their Fish up,
And trudg'd away to cry *No Bishop*.
The *Mouse-trap* men laid *Save-alls* by,
And 'gainst *Ev'l Counsellors* did cry.[2]

The category of 'burlesque' does not throw any light on such
a passage. One is reminded, rather, that Butler has no serious
rival between Jonson and Crabbe as a realistic poet of low
life. To match his description of the astrologer's zany—

His bus'ness was to pump and wheedle,
And Men with their own keys unriddle.
To make them to themselves give answers,
For which they pay the *Necromancers*.
To fetch and carry *Intelligence*,
Of whom, and what, and where, and whence.

.   .   .

Draw *Figures*, *Schemes*, and *Horoscopes*,
Of *Newgate*, *Bridewell*, *Brokers* Shops.

[1] p. 144 (II. ii. 585–92 and 601–4).
[2] p. 42 (I. ii. 535–42).

> Of Thieves *ascendent* in the *Cart*,
> And find out all by rules of *Art*.
> Which way a Serving-man that's run
> With Cloaths or Mony away, is gone:
> Who pick'd a *Fob*, at *Holding-forth*,
> And where a *Watch*, for half the worth,
> May be redeem'd; or Stolen Plate
> Restor'd, at Conscionable rate;[1]

—to match this one must go to Defoe's descriptions of rogues and vagabonds.[2]

Although the set 'character' is less prominent in Butler's satire than in that of Dryden or Pope, it plays no unimportant part; as we should expect of the man who wrote such witty prose 'characters', these portraits in verse are brilliantly done:

> Fast Friend he was to *Reformation*,
> Until 'twas worn quite out of fashion.
> Next Rectifier of Wry *Law*,
> And would make three, to cure one flaw.
> Learned he was, and could take note,
> Transcribe, Collect, Translate and Quote.
> But *Preaching* was his chiefest Talent,
> Or Argument, in which b'ing valiant,
> He us'd to lay about and stickle,
> Like *Ram* or *Bull*, at *Conventicle*:
> For Disputants like *Rams* and *Bulls*,
> Do fight with *Arms* that spring from *Skulls*.[3]

There is no doubt that Butler was one of Dryden's principal masters in the art of satire. 'The worth of his poem is too well known to need my commendation', Dryden remarked, 'and he is above my censure.'[4] It is interesting to compare the 'character' of Shaftesbury in *Hudibras* with the well-known sketch in *Absalom and Achitophel*:

---

[1] pp. 160–1 (II. iii. 335–40 and 347–56).
[2] See, for example, Defoe's description of a 'magician' at Bristol Fair, in *A System of Magick* (1727), pp. 560 et seq.
[3] p. 39 (I. ii. 429–40).
[4] *Essays*, ii. 105.

'Mong these there was a *Politician*,
With more Heads then a *Beast in Vision*,
And more Intrigues in ev'ry one
Then all the *Whores of Babylon*;
So politick, as if one eye
Upon the other were a Spy;

. . . .

Could turn his Word, and Oath, and Faith,
As many ways as in a Lath;
By turning, wriggle, like a Screw
Int' highest Trust, and out for New.[1]

Butler's 'character' is in the 'low' style, as against Dryden's
heroic portraiture;[2] he makes no pretence of impartiality;
his aim is frankly that of the caricaturist. Butler's 'character'
of the Presbyterians, finally, is particularly reminiscent of
Dryden:

A Sect, whose chief Devotion lies
In odd perverse Antipathies;
In falling out with that or this,
And finding somewhat still amiss.

. . . .

Still so perverse and opposite,
As if they worshipp'd God for spight,
The self-same thing they will abhor
One way, and long another for.[3]

One is reminded of the apostrophe to the 'Almighty crowd'
that shortens all dispute in *The Medal*.[4] Butler resembled
Dryden in despising the crowd, and fearing it. 'I do not
remember in all History', he wrote in one of his notebooks,
'any one good thing that ever was don by the People, in any
government, but millions of bad ones.'[5] Butler's satire on
Dissent is inspired by fear of the mob. This 'anti-democratic'
note came to be almost a constant characteristic of the best in
Augustan satire.

[1] pp. 248–9 (III. ii. 351–6 and 375–8).
[2] See pp. 67–68 below. But compare the much 'lower' portrait of Shaftesbury in *The Medal*, which is nearer to Butler—particularly in its use of imagery (pp. 67 n.–68 n. below).
[3] pp. 8–9 (I. i. 207–10 and 217–20).
[4] ll. 91 et seq.   [5] *Characters*, p. 371.

Butler's distinction is twofold. He took over a traditional manner of 'low' writing and used it with a brilliance and variety of effect which were new things, and which led Dennis to call him 'a whole Species of Poets in one'.[1] And, secondly, he differed from earlier burlesque writers in using this amazing idiom 'with a just design, which was to expose Hypocrisie'.[2] So doing, Butler was true to his own ideal of satire: 'A Satyr', he wrote, 'is a kinde of Knight Errant that goe's upon Adventures, to Relieve the Distressed Damsel Virtue, and Redeeme Honour out of Inchanted Castles, And opprest Truth, and Reason out of the Captivity of Gyants or Magitians.'[3] By adapting burlesque to the fundamental requirement of decorum, a worthy and unifying 'end', Butler was able to write one of the greatest comic poems in the language.

[1] *Remarks upon Mr. Pope's Translation of Homer* (1717), in Hooker, ii. 121.
[2] Preface to *Miscellanies in Verse and Prose* (1693), in Hooker, i. 7.
[3] *Characters*, p. 469.

III

MOCK-HEROIC: *MACFLECKNOE*

*Il n'y a rien . . . de plus ridicule que de raconter une histoire comique
et absurde en termes graves et sérieux.*

BOILEAU[1]

'MORE libels have been written against me', Dryden
remarked in the *Discourse concerning the Original
and Progress of Satire*, 'than almost any man now
living. . . . But let the world witness for me, that . . . I have
seldom answered any scurrilous lampoon, when it was in my
power to have exposed my enemies: and, being naturally
vindicative, have suffered in silence, and possessed my soul
in quiet.'[2] If we accept Johnson's definition of a lampoon as
'a personal satire; abuse; censure written not to reform but
to vex', we must admit that the fundamental impulse behind
MacFlecknoe is that of the lampooner. It is so evidently inspired by no wish to reform Shadwell, or to reform anyone,
that it sets a problem for the moral apologist for satire.
Dryden felt this difficulty when he came to write his own
essay on satire, and was forced to conclude that a lampoon is
'a dangerous sort of weapon, and for the most part unlawful.
We have no moral right on the reputation of other men. 'Tis
taking from them what we cannot restore to them.'[3]

The immediate occasion of *MacFlecknoe* is uncertain. No
doubt Dryden felt that he had been 'notoriously abused'—
which he allows as a partial exculpation for writing a lampoon. All that is definitely known is that during the year
1678 something acted as a match to the heaped-up straw of
Dryden's contempt for Shadwell and set him writing the
only poem in his work which is wholly devoted to satirizing
a private enemy. It is noteworthy that Dryden confines
himself to Shadwell's literary character; in spite of the

---

[1] *Dissertation sur Joconde* (1669).   [2] *Essays*, ii. 80.
[3] Ibid. ii. 79.

misleading sub-title, *A Satyr upon the True-Blew-Protestant Poet, T. S.*,[1] nothing is said of Shadwell's religious or political opinions; nor is his moral character seriously attacked. Dryden confines himself to portraying him as a literary dunce. The words 'wit', 'sense', 'art', 'nature', 'nonsense', 'tautology', and 'dulness', which had been the current coin of Dryden's prolonged critical warfare with Shadwell, sound through the poem like a fanfare.

In its original impulse, then, *MacFlecknoe* may be considered as a lampoon. Dryden also described it as a Varronian satire, a category for which its primary qualification seems to be that it is based on a story of the poet's own invention. But the most helpful classification of the poem, as well as the most familiar, is that of the mock-heroic. Faced with the task of making Shadwell ridiculous, Dryden chose as his method the ironical politeness of the mock-epic.

MacFlecknoe is highly original. There are several English poems, of which the *Nun's Priest's Tale* is the least unlikely, which may have given Dryden a hint. But there is no earlier poem in the language which is at all comparable with it as a whole. The manner of the greatest satirist of the previous age, already cheapened by a host of imitators, was unacceptable to Dryden. When he remarks that Boileau 'had read the burlesque poetry of Scarron, with some kind of indignation, as witty as it was',[2] the parallel with his own attitude to Butler is unmistakable. Dryden aspired to write 'manly satire' and felt that the style of *Hudibras* 'turns earnest too much to jest, and gives us a boyish kind of pleasure'.[3] Believing satire 'undoubtedly a species' of heroic poetry,[4] he had to look elsewhere for a model which would teach him how to give weight to his censure. He found what he wanted in *Le Lutrin*. 'This, I think . . . to be the most beautiful, and most noble kind of satire', he was later to sum up. 'Here is the majesty of the heroic, finely mixed with the venom of

---

[1] This was no doubt added by the publisher of the first edition, which seems to have been pirated. See Hugh Macdonald, *John Dryden: A Bibliography* (1939), p. 30.

[2] *Essays*, ii. 107.   [3] Ibid. ii. 105.

[4] Ibid. ii. 108.

the other; and raising the delight which otherwise would be flat and vulgar, by the sublimity of the expression.'[1]

II

Fully to appreciate the use of a mock-heroic idiom for highly uncomplimentary purposes it is necessary to be familiar with the panegyrical use of the heroic style. Fortunately the approach to *MacFlecknoe* is rendered easy by the fact that many passages of *Absalom and Achitophel* exemplify the use of the heroic style for panegyric which is here parodied. Any misconception of the modern reader's that a mock-heroic poem is designed to ridicule the heroic genre, or that it will be written in a bombastic, ranting style, is removed by a glance at *MacFlecknoe*. Dryden does not, like Pope's Blackmore,

> Rend with tremendous Sound [our] ears asunder,
> With Gun, Drum, Trumpet, Blunderbuss & Thunder.[2]

On the contrary a reader who did not know both poems well would be at a loss to say which of the following passages belonged to the heroic poem, which to the mock-heroic:

> (*a*) This aged Prince now flourishing in Peace,
> And blest with issue of a large increase,
> Worn out with business, did at length debate
> To settle the Succession of the State.

> (*b*) With secret Joy, indulgent *David* view'd
> His Youthful Image in his Son renew'd;
> To all his wishes Nothing he deni'd
> And made the Charming *Annabel* his Bride.[3]

The style of many passages in *MacFlecknoe* is identical with the polished heroic idiom of *Absalom and Achitophel*. The joke that makes it 'a poem exquisitely satirical'[4] consists in

---

[1] Ibid. For an examination of Dryden's debt to *Le Lutrin* see A. F. B. Clark's *Boileau and the French Classical Critics in England* (1925), particularly pp. 156–8.

[2] *The First Satire of the Second Book of Horace*, ll. 25–26.

[3] (*a*) *MacFlecknoe*, ll. 7–10; (*b*) *Absalom*, ll. 31–34. All quotations in this chapter and the next are from *The Poems of John Dryden*, Oxford edition, ed. John Sargeaunt (1913).

[4] Johnson's *Lives*, i. 383.

using this style, which was soon to prove a perfect medium
for a poem about the King and weighty matters of State, to
describe Shadwell and his insignificant affairs. Nor is Shadwell so insignificant before Dryden gets to work: it is the
elevated style that makes him so. A small man is not in
himself a ridiculous object: he becomes ridiculous when he
is dressed up in a suit of armour designed for a hero. The
discrepancy between the important matters that the style is
continually suggesting and the question of Flecknoe's successor is so marked that a shock of laughter ensues.

The purpose of such a poem must be made clear, as
wittily as possible, right from the start. Here Dryden suc-
ceeds perfectly, striking the full mock-heroic note with a
grave *sententia*:

> All humane things are subject to decay,
> And, when Fate summons, Monarchs must obey.

These lines might form the opening of a panegyrical funeral
elegy on a royal personage; but the direction of the *prosecutio*
which follows indicates the mock-heroic intention beyond all
doubt:

> This *Fleckno* found.[1]

Right from the start, too, we have 'the numbers of heroic
poesy', which emphasize by their harmonious dignity the ludi-
crousness of the matter. Triplets, usually a sign of increased
elevation in Dryden, are used with similar effect:

> For ancient *Decker* prophesi'd long since, ⎫
> That in this Pile should Reign a mighty Prince, ⎬
> Born for a scourge of Wit, and flayle of Sense.[2] ⎭

The skilful manner in which Dryden mingles direct and
oblique attack is particularly clear in Flecknoe's speeches,
which are introduced and terminated with due heightening
of style and make up more than half of the poem. In a direct
lampoon the lines

---

[1] Compare the much 'lower' sententious passage, 36 lines long, followed by the usual
prosecutio ('This Hudibras by proof found true'), with which *Hudibras*, ii. iii begins.
[2] ll. 87–89.

> The rest to some faint meaning make pretence,
> But *Shadwell* never deviates into sense,[1]

would be severe enough. They are rendered lethal by being uttered as an encomium.

One of the characteristics of the heroic idiom which Dryden adapts to his own purpose is the dignified *descriptio* of time and place. The great event is ushered in by a formal passage:

> Now Empress Fame had publisht the renown
> Of *Shadwell's* Coronation through the Town.
> Rows'd by report of Fame, the Nations meet,
> From near *Bun-hill* and distant *Watling-street*. . . .[2]

The scene of the solemnity is described with equal pomp:

> Close to the Walls which fair *Augusta* bind,
> (The fair *Augusta* much to fears inclin'd)
> An ancient fabrick rais'd t'inform the sight,
> There stood of yore, and *Barbican* it hight.[3]

In these passages the mock-heroic application of methods of description familiar in classical literature to scenes of contemporary 'low' life is a reminder of the realistic bias of Dryden's mind—a bias characteristic of much of the best Augustan poetry.[4] He is very successful in his delineation of the 'low' quarters of the town, 'brothel-houses', and the haunts of 'the suburbian Muse'. The whole background of the poem (and not least the trap-door at the end, which parodies the heavy humour of Shadwell's play *The Virtuoso*) is reminiscent of the setting of a low comedy or farce. To remember Shadwell's dramatic propensities is to relish the poetic justice of the joke.

'As Virgil in his fourth Georgic, of the Bees, perpetually raises the lowness of his subject, by the loftiness of his words', Dryden observes in his remarks on *Le Lutrin*, 'and ennobles

---

[1] ll. 19–20. Here and elsewhere Sargeaunt follows the early editions in reading '*Sh——*'.
[2] ll. 94–97.   [3] ll. 64–67.
[4] This device became essential to the 'Augustan Eclogue', a descriptive piece modelled on the classical eclogue which dealt with the urban scene in a highly realistic manner. See p. 149 below.

it by comparisons drawn from empires, and from monarchs
. . . we see Boileau pursuing him in the same flights, and
scarcely yielding to his master.'[1] The mock-heroic imagery
of *MacFlecknoe* is no less brilliant. The joyful business of
comparing small men to giants and making pygmies of them
in the process begins in the third line of the poem, where we
hear that Flecknoe,

> . . . like *Augustus*, young
> Was call'd to Empire and had govern'd long.[2]

The unfortunate Shadwell is compared in turn to Arion, to
'young *Ascanius* . . . *Rome*'s other hope and Pillar of the
State', to Hannibal, and to '*Romulus* . . . by *Tyber*'s *Brook*'.[3]
The tendency to blasphemy which is never far away in
Dryden, whether in satire or panegyric, becomes very marked
in the account of the signs and omens which foreshadowed
Shadwell's coming. Flecknoe's speech parodies John the
Baptist's:

> *Heywood* and *Shirley* were but Types of thee,
> Thou last great Prophet of Tautology:
> Even I, a dunce of more renown than they,
> Was sent before but to prepare thy way:
> And coarsely clad in *Norwich* Drugget came
> To teach the Nations in thy greater name.[4]

The manner in which the mantle of Flecknoe falls on the
shoulders of Shadwell recalls the case of Elijah, who left the
earth in the other direction.

It is not only in mock-heroic imagery (imagery which
diminishes by irony) that *MacFlecknoe* excels. Brilliant
examples of direct satirical imagery may also be found,
notably in the latter part of Flecknoe's second speech, which
makes relatively little use of irony and is written in a style
closer to that of direct satire than most other parts of the
poem:

> When did his Muse from *Fletcher* scenes purloin,
> As thou whole Eth'ridg dost transfuse to thine?

---

[1] *Essays*, ii. 107–8.   [2] ll. 3–4.
[3] ll. 43, 108–9, 112–13, 130–1.   [4] ll. 29–34.

But so transfused as Oyls on Waters flow,
His always floats above, thine sinks below.
This is thy Province, this thy wondrous way,
New Humours to invent for each new Play:
This is that boasted Byas of thy mind,
By which one way, to dullness, 'tis inclined,
Which makes thy writings lean on one side still,
And, in all changes, that way bends thy will.[1]
Nor let thy mountain belly make pretence
Of likeness; thine's a tympany[2] of sense.
A Tun of Man in thy large Bulk is writ,
But sure thou'rt but a Kilderkin of wit.[3]

In such a passage the satire is wholly conveyed by the images. Starting with the simple object of name-calling, the poet chooses an image: as he gives expression to it another starts up in his mind, and the new image is tossed about until a third presents itself to his attention. The result is satire of great power: satire which differs completely—one may note in passing—from anything in *Le Lutrin*.

III

One of the passages in the *Discourse concerning ... Satire* most frequently quoted and applied to Dryden's own satiric method occurs in the section devoted to complimenting the Earl of Dorset and Middlesex.

How easy is it to call rogue and villain, and that wittily! But how hard to make a man appear a fool, a blockhead, or a knave, without using any of those opprobrious terms! To spare the grossness of the names, and to do the thing yet more severely, is to draw a full face, and to

---

[1] As has often been pointed out, these lines parody a passage from the epilogue to Shadwell's *The Humorists*:

> A Humor is the Byas of the Mind,
> By which with violence 'tis one way inclin'd:
> It makes our Actions lean on one side still,
> And in all Changes that way bends the Will. (15–18.)

The parody is particularly appropriate because Ben Jonson was the focus of most of the disputes between Dryden and Shadwell.

[2] 'A kind of obstructed flatulence that swells the body like a drum.' Johnson.

[3] 183–96 ('Kilderkin' = a small barrel of wine, contrasting with 'Tun').

make the nose and cheeks stand out, and yet not to employ any depth
of shadowing. This is the mystery of that noble trade, which yet no
master can teach to his apprentice. . . . There is . . . a vast difference
betwixt the slovenly butchering of a man, and the fineness of a stroke
that separates the head from the body, and leaves it standing in its place.
A man may be capable, as Jack Ketch's wife said of his servant, of a
plain piece of work, a bare hanging; but to make a malefactor die
sweetly was only belonging to her husband.[1]

In spite of this praise of indirectness in satire, however,
Dryden cannot conceal the fact that he prefers the direct
Juvenal to the indirect Horace. Admitting that 'the manner
of Juvenal' is inferior to that of Horace, he claims that
'Juvenal has excelled him in his performance. Juvenal has
railed more wittily than Horace has rallied.'[2] Indirectness
is not the most striking characteristic of Dryden's own
satire. While 'raillery' is perhaps a better word to describe
MacFlecknoe than 'railing', the obliquity of the attack can
easily be exaggerated. The fundamental irony is the mock-
heroic conception of the whole, and the brilliant heroic
idiom in which it is written. The ridicule is much more
direct than that in *A Tale of a Tub* or *Jonathan Wild the
Great*. Qualities in fact ridiculous are nominally praised;
but they are given their true names, 'dulness', 'nonsense',
'tautology'. Dryden does not tell us that Shadwell is a great
poet, as Fielding tells us that Wild is a great man. Instead,
and with the greatest gusto, he hammers out his lines of
magnificent abuse:

> Success let others teach, learn thou from me
> Pangs without birth, and fruitless Industry.[3]

That Dryden is at liberty to speak out in this way is largely
due to the fact that the heroic idiom is continually asserting
that the hero is a great man, in a manner in which no prose
style would be powerful enough to do. Helped by the
'ostentation' of the verse (to borrow a good term from Charles
Williams), Dryden is at liberty to use direct abuse without

---

[1] *Essays*, ii. 92–93.   [2] Ibid. 94–95.
[3] ll. 147–8.

being inartistic. This is particularly evident in the speeches. The reader enjoys hearing Shadwell being abused without feeling that he is assisting in an unmannerly brawl; and the elevation of the verse adds authority to the condemnation. This mingling of irony with direct abuse is more effective than pure irony.

In writing *MacFlecknoe* Dryden had no intention of ridiculing his own heroic style, of which the greatest example still lay before him, or the heroic poem as a genre. If 'parody' is taken, as in modern usage it often is, to mean a composition which ridicules the style of a given poet or poetic kind by exaggeration (as in Swinburne's self-parodies), then *MacFlecknoe* is innocent of parodic intention; except that one or two touches—principally the conclusion, and the archaisms 'whilom', 'hight', and 'yore'—ridicule the manner of Flecknoe, Shadwell, and bad poets in general. But if by parody is meant 'a kind of writing, in which the words of an author or his thoughts are taken, and by a slight change adapted to some new purpose',[1] several parodic passages may be found. They are not intended to ridicule their originals, but merely—as in the lines about the 'Mother-Strumpets',[2] which parody Cowley—to amuse the reader by the allusion, and by the contrast between the original subject of the passage and that to which it is now applied. The elements of parody in *MacFlecknoe* are simply specific instances of the mock-heroic conception of the whole poem.[3]

Appreciation of the devastating satire of *MacFlecknoe* should not be allowed to blind us to its sheer comedy. It is one of the few poems that Dryden wrote for his own satisfaction, and there is no doubt that he enjoyed himself. His delight is evident everywhere, in the brilliant imagery lavished on Shadwell—

> His goodly Fabrick fills the eye
> And seems design'd for thoughtless Majesty:

---

[1] Johnson's *Dictionary*.   [2] ll. 72–73.

[3] 'Parody' is only one of the critical terms which have changed their meaning since the Augustan age. To investigate the meaning of some of these words is one of the objects of this study.

> Thoughtless as Monarch Oakes that shade the plain,
> And, spread in solemn state, supinely reign[1]

—or in the hilarious couplet of advice which Flecknoe bestows on his successor:

> Let Father *Flecknoe* fire thy mind with praise
> *And Uncle Ogleby thy envy raise.*[2]

Throughout the poem there is an element of imaginative fantasy surpassed in *The Rape of the Lock* but lacking in many parts of the *Dunciad*. Shadwell is a *creation* in a sense in which Cibber is not. *MacFlecknoe* is not only a satire: it is also a comedy. Mere scorn withers. It is the ironic sympathy in Dryden's poem, the mischievous joy in contemplation, that gives life to a creature of the comic imagination. Shadwell takes his place as a member of the same company as Sir John Falstaff himself.

---

[1] ll. 25–28.
[2] ll. 173–4. (My italics.)

IV

A WITTY HEROIC POEM:
ABSALOM AND ACHITOPHEL

*A moral composition to represent the good and ill effects of different
characters and passions.*

H. PEMBERTON[1]

As Dryden admits in the preface, *Absalom and Achitophel*
is a party poem. In 1681 a crisis occurred in the
conflict between Shaftesbury and his followers, who
wished to exclude the Catholic Duke of York from succession to the throne, and those who stood with the King himself
in favour of 'true succession'. Towards the end of the year
Shaftesbury was to be brought before a Grand Jury, and
Dryden was asked, probably by the King himself, to write
a poem in opposition to the flood of pamphlets stating the
Whig case.[2] The publication of *Absalom and Achitophel* about
the middle of November was no doubt timed to influence
Shaftesbury's trial.

What Dryden did was to write a narrative poem describing
the events which had led up to the present situation in the
manner in which the King's followers wanted them to be
viewed. His profession of impartiality is unconvincing: the
picture which he paints is the official picture. The political
intention of the poem is emphasized by the fact that the
concluding speech from the throne summarizes several of the
arguments put forward in the official defence of the dissolu-
tions of Parliament.[3]

[1] Definition of a heroic poem in *Observations on Poetry, Especially the Epic: Occasioned by
the Late Poem upon Leonidas* (1738), p. 4.

[2] A note prefixed to the 1716 edition of *The Second Part of Absalom and Achitophel* (which
is mainly the work of Nahum Tate) is our authority for believing that Dryden's poem was
undertaken 'upon the desire of King Charles the Second'. Whether the King indicated the
sort of poem he wanted or left the choice to Dryden is unknown.

[3] In 'The Conclusion of Dryden's Absalom and Achitophel', *H.L.Q.* Nov. 1946, Mr.
Godfrey Davies has shown that it was not Charles's speech to the Oxford Parliament that
Dryden summarized, as used to be supposed, but *His Majesties Declaration to all His Loving
Subjects Touching the Causes and Reasons that moved Him to Dissolve the two last Parliaments.*

II

What may be regarded as a standard justification of the use of allegory in a political composition is to be found in Barclay's *Argenis*, an account of the affairs of France during the religious wars which Dryden is sure to have known.[1] The author of this work, which was published in 1621 and dedicated to Louis XIII, describes his purpose in these words:

I will compile some stately Fable, in manner of a History ... Then will I with the shew of danger stirre vp pitty, feare, and horrour: and by and by cheere vp all doubts, and graciously allay the tempests. Whom I please, I will deliuer, and whom I please, giue vp to the Fates. I know the disposition of our Countrey-men: because I seeme to tell them Tales, I shall haue them all ... While they reade, while they are affected with anger or fauour, as it were against strangers, they shall meete with themselves; and finde in the glasse held before them, the shew and merit of their owne fame. It will perchance make them ashamed longer to play those parts vpon the stage of this life, for which they must confesse themselves iustly taxed in a fable.[2]

After the publication of d'Urfé's *Astrée* the fashion for allegory became so widespread in France that every fictitious work was scrutinized for its political significance. 'Their readers persisted in considering them merely as *histoires travesties*, relating, under assumed names, all that had happened or was taking place at Court or in the nation at large.'[3] Allegory was particularly prominent in the hundreds of *Mazarinades* or pamphlets against Cardinal Mazarin which appeared during the troubles of the Fronde. In England, too, the use of political allegory increased greatly during the civil war and the controversies which succeeded it. Charles and his courtiers brought a taste for this species of writing

Published by His Majesties Command (1681). Dryden wrote a prose pamphlet, *His Majesties Declaration Defended*, which appeared in June of the same year. (Reprinted by the Augustan Reprint Society, 1950.)

[1] Dryden mentions Barclay's *Euphormio* as an example of Varronian satire. *Essays*, ii. 67.

[2] *Barclay His Argenis*, translated by Kingesmill Long (1625), Lib. 2, Cap. 14 (p. 109).

[3] Archimede Marni, *Allegory in the French Heroic Poetry of the Seventeenth Century* (1936), p. 49.

with them from France; and there can be little doubt that
the pamphleteers who attacked Shaftesbury, Dryden among
them, looked into such French productions as came their
way in search of hints that would help in the composition of
their own lampoons and satires.

Two English allegorical poems seem to have afforded
Dryden suggestions. *Naboth's Vinyard: or, the Innocent
Traytor* (1679) was described by Luttrell as 'a Popish Libell
design'd agt ye Judge, and the witnesses in the late plott'.[1]
The anonymous production of a little-known writer called
John Caryll, it resembles *Absalom and Achitophel* in being a
narrative poem in heroic couplets in which an Old Testament
allegory is used to describe contemporary events as they
appear to a partisan. The style is heroic, and the narrative
is interspersed with reflective and exclamatory passages,
speeches, and 'characters' of the *dramatis personae*. One or
two brief passages from this poem are quoted on a later page.[2]

While the influence of *Naboth's Vinyard* on *Absalom and
Achitophel* has often been pointed out, that of *The Progress
of Honesty*, which appeared the year after Caryll's satire,
seems to have been overlooked.[3] In this poem of some 850
lines D'Urfey describes the rebellion of 'the long Ear'd rout'
against Titus the Second, a king of 'God-like Clemency':

> What Vertue ere did Heaven to man impart,
> That centers not within his Royal Heart?[4]

Most of the King's party are described by classical or
Italianate names—Parmenio, Clitus, Cleon, Memnon, Bat-
tus, Mecenas, Villanio—while many of Shaftesbury's followers (though not Monmouth himself) are given names
drawn from the Old Testament. Some people call Shaftesbury
Hophni, some Achitophel,

> Others chief Advocate for Hell;[5]

---

[1] Macdonald, p. 214.   [2] p. 74 n.

[3] I am indebted to Col. C. H. Wilkinson for this discovery. *The Progress of Honesty* bears
the date 1681 on the title-page, but Luttrell's copy, in the possession of Col. Wilkinson, is
dated 11 October 1680.

[4] st. viii, ll. 13–14.   [5] st. xiv, l. 9.

the people are the Israelites; and there are references to Rabbis, '*Ashteroth* and *Moloch*, Idols famous known', and Gog and Magog. The description of Monmouth is a foreshadowing of Dryden's Absalom:

> In this impetuous Torrent of the State,
>   Young *Marcian* rises, fam'd of late
> For Conduct, Courage, and Advantages of Fate,
> Mighty in Office, Publick in Report,
> Powerful in th'Army, and Belov'd at Court,
> Born on the Peoples Shoulders with such Pride,
> As Indian Kings on conquer'd Princes ride;
> Heaven markt him for uncommon Dignity,
> None Favour'd more, nor none more Great than he,
> Till Hells curst Agents caus'd his Sense to stray,
> Out of his oncelov'd Path, his Loyal Way,
>   And counsell'd him to disobey.[1]

In the end there is forgiveness:

> With joyful look the Sire his Convert grac'd,
> Thrice blest the kneeling Youth, and thrice embrac'd;
> And as the Kingly Prophet once did *Absalom*,
> Forgave his sins of youth, caress'd and brought him home.

But the resemblances between *The Progress of Honesty* and *Absalom and Achitophel* are less striking than they sound in analysis. D'Urfey's 'View of a Court and City'—to quote the sub-title—has affinities with the Vision type of satire used by Oldham and others. Dryden's direct opening is much preferable to D'Urfey's fiction that the poet, reclining in a lonely grove on an evening in summer, overhears Honesty narrating the circumstances of the plot to his son Error. Another difference between the two poems is the mingling in *The Progress of Honesty* of such abstract characters as Faction, 'Old Discord', and 'pale-Fac't Treason' with the characters from the contemporary political scene: it is Error, not Marcian, who is forgiven in the lines quoted above. Most important of all is the contrast between Dryden's skilful couplets and the discursive 'pindariques' of D'Urfey.

---

[1] st. xi, ll. 1–12.

D'Urfey's unfortunate choice of metre greatly detracts from the value of his poem.[1]

The particular allegory on which *Absalom and Achitophel* is based was neither Dryden's invention nor D'Urfey's.[2] Steeped in Scripture by his hated 'Scotch Divines', Charles likened himself to David early in his reign. The wit of the comparison was not its only recommendation. Charles had in mind the morals drawn from the story of David by contemporary preachers: 'Let no man look to prosper by rebellion', and 'How easily may the fickle multitude be transported to the wrong side.'[3] To loyal subjects of the King the story of David seemed only 'too fit a patterne for the present times'.[4] It was quite natural that when Nathaniel Lee urged Dryden to celebrate the sufferings and triumph of the King he should have mentioned Cowley's treatment of David as a model:

> Monarch of verse! new themes employ thy pen.
> The troubles of majestic Charles set down;
> Not David vanquished more to reach a crown.
> Praise him as Cowley did that Hebrew king:
> Thy theme's as great; do thou as greatly sing.[5]

The analogy between David's indulgent attitude to his son and Charles's to Monmouth was so obvious that it may well be, as has recently been suggested, that what Dryden needed

---

[1] Some passages of *The Progress of Honesty* are reminiscent of *Hudibras*—

> And as *Venetians* deal with Jews,
> Commit it carefully to use   (st. xv, ll. 7–8)

—others of Dryden:

> Hark how the *Mobile* shout, that ecchoing peal
> Portends the downfal of some Common-Weal.   (st. v, ll. 25–26)

> For he this thriving Maxim has profest,
> That th' Conscience of the Wise is interest;
> But that in proper time a Bank might swell,
> To bribe dissenting Brethren to rebel.   (st. xv, ll. 11–14.)

[2] Earlier examples of the same allegory are mentioned in the Scott-Saintsbury ed. of Dryden's *Works* (1882–92), ix. 198 et seq., and in R. F. Jones's 'The Originality of *Absalom and Achitophel*' (*M.L.N.* April 1931).

[3] Joseph Hall, *Works* (Oxford, 1837), i. 443. Cited by Davies.

[4] Part of the title of *Absalom's Rebellion . . .*, published at Oxford in 1645. Cited by Davies.

[5] Commendatory Verses to *The State of Innocence* (1677). S.-S. v. 110.

was not the idea but 'permission or encouragement to use it'.[1]

What is most remarkable is the way in which Dryden used the allegory. Although a contemporary subject must have had many attractions for a poet who shared Milton's desire for subjects of unassailable truth,[2] there were serious difficulties in the way of investing it with any degree of grandeur. As Davenant had pointed out in his discussion of the heroic poem, 'men, even of the best education, discover their eyes to be weak when they look upon the glory of Vertue, which is great actions, and rather endure it at distance then neer, being more apt to beleeve and love the renown of Predecessors then of Contemporaries, whose deeds, excelling theirs in their own sight, seem to upbraid them, and are not reverenc'd as examples of Vertue, but envy'd as the favours of Fortune'.[3] Envy apart, the familiarity of the subject-matter was against the poet. As Verrall remarked, such unavoidable words as *Parliament*, *Jury*, *writ*, and *committee* defy an elevated idiom;[4] they would have reduced Dryden's poem to the mock-heroic level, precisely as *Fleckno*, *Ogleby*, and *Shadwell* reduce *MacFlecknoe*. The Old Testament allegory helped Dryden to raise his poem to a dignified level without collapsing into bathos.

The possibility of using an elevated style was not the only benefit conferred by the allegory.[5] It also acted as the

---

[1] Davies, p. 70.

[2] 'Intolerance of all except what seemed to him *most real* was ... a characteristic of Milton which linked him with his age, and vitally affected his choice of poetic subject.' Basil Willey, *The Seventeenth Century Background* (1934), p. 227. (Willey's italics.)

[3] Preface to *Gondibert*, in Spingarn, ii. 11.

[4] *Lectures on Dryden* (1914), pp. 56–57.

[5] Together, the allegory and the elevated style of *Absalom and Achitophel* may be regarded as the equivalent of a dignified Latin idiom. Although it would by no means have served Dryden's purpose, which was to reach as wide a public as possible, it was still quite common to write 'heroic' poems on contemporary events in Latin. (Cf. pp. 11 et seq., above, and see Leicester Bradner's 'Poems on the Defeat of the Spanish Armada' (*J.E.G.P.* Oct. 1944), as well as his book.) As mentioned above, schoolboys (and no doubt Dryden among them) were required to write on such topics as 'The Fifth of November'. Elaborate descriptions and forensic speeches were common features in such poems, as was a debate in Hell. Like the debate in Book II of *Paradise Lost*, *Absalom and Achitophel* may owe a few hints to exercises of this sort.

instrument of Dryden's brilliant wit, and helped to give
the poem an air of objectivity more impressive than the
direct exclamatoriness so common in political satire. Because
it is misleadingly over-simplified, the action stands out in
relief; and the fact that such figures as The King, The
Tempter, and The Mob are so readily recognized carries
the action a step further from the realm of mere political
wrangling in the direction of universal philosophical or
poetic truth.

Dryden despised mere lampooners and had no intention
of allowing a poem on which he would have to bestow a great
deal of effort to remain on the same low level as the majority
of the productions of the 'violent paper scuffle'[1] to which it
was a contribution. In the allegory which he took over and
remodelled he found a powerful ally in the task of raising
political satire to the level of high art.[2]

III

Although *Absalom and Achitophel* has always been known
as a satire, the style in which it is written is by no means
a characteristically satiric idiom. The object of Dryden's
first official production as Laureate is not merely to attack
the men who plotted against the King, but to present the
whole constitutional position to the reader in a certain way.
While the King's enemies are represented in an unfavourable

Such poems would usually be written in Latin epic style, Virgil being the model. It is only
to be expected, therefore, that in writing such a poem in English the poet would tend to write as
'heroically' as he could—subject to such qualifications as the nature of his purpose suggested.

The importance to Dryden of Virgilian inspiration has been emphasized by Reuben Arthur
Brower in 'Dryden's Epic Manner' (*P.M.L.A.* Mar. 1940).

[1] Luttrell's phrase, quoted by Macdonald, p. 19.

[2] Two articles by Weldon M. Williams—'The Genesis of John Oldham's *Satyrs Upon
the Jesuits*' (*P.M.L.A.* Dec. 1943) and 'The Influence of Ben Jonson's *Catiline* upon John
Oldham's *Satyrs Upon the Jesuits*' (*E.L.H.* Mar. 1944)—are of interest to the student of
Dryden because they examine the models which a satirist had for his guidance at this time.
As Williams points out, both Dryden and Oldham were searching for a dignified vehicle for
their satire. But his remark that while 'Oldham's poems are in a falsely inflated style . . .
Dryden's stayed much closer to the idiom and atmosphere of the lampoon or libel, even while
reacting against it as a form' (*P.M.L.A.*, p. 970) is misleading. Oldham used an unsuccessful
heroic style, while Dryden scored a signal success with an original blending of the heroic with
the witty.

light, the Royal party is eulogistically portrayed. It is appropriate, therefore, that the idiom is not the middle or low style of lampoon or the commonest sorts of denigrating satire, but a basically heroic style[1] with occasional base details in the portraits of Shaftesbury's followers.

If the celebrated 'characters' of Achitophel, Zimri, and the rest are set on one side until the poem as a whole has been brought into focus, it becomes evident that *Absalom and Achitophel* is much closer in style to Cowley's *Davideis* than to *Hudibras* or Pope's *Imitations of Horace*. Like an epic or a heroic play Dryden's poem represents 'Nature wrought up to an higher pitch'; as a natural consequence 'the plot, the characters, the wit, the passions, the descriptions, are all exalted above the level of common converse, as high as the imagination of the poet can carry them, with proportion to verisimility'.[2]

The verse of *Absalom and Achitophel* is marked by what Dryden called 'the Smoothness, the Numbers, and the Turn of Heroique Poetry'.[3] Instead of the radical enjambements and feminine rhymes common in the lower species of poetry

---

[1] In the Renaissance itself and (to a much greater degree) ever since, the term 'heroic verse' has led to a great deal of confusion. Since by 'heroic couplets' we now mean nothing more than a metrical form, irrespective of every other aspect of the idiom, the fact that 'heroic verse' has as its proper meaning 'a *style* suitable for a heroic poem' has been forgotten. Quite early 'heroic verse' was occasionally used with a purely metrical connotation; but in its normal use it was intimately connected with the theory of the levels of style. Whereas we stress 'heroic *verse*' (= metre), Renaissance writers usually stressed '*heroic* verse' (poetic style). The fact that 'heroic' referred to the whole idiom is emphasized by the existence of the term 'Heroic prose' (Pope, *Epistle to Arbuthnot*, l. 109).

A remarkable result of this confusion is the modern delusion that all poems written in 'heroic couplets' (or at least end-stopped couplets) are in much the same style. The recurrent rhyme has such a hypnotic effect on the untrained reader that he becomes oblivious of every other aspect of the style.

In fact, of course, a number of poems all written in 'heroic couplets' may be in very different styles. Compare, for instance, the quotations on pp. 62 n. 2, 64, 83–84, 111–12, and 139 of this study.

The modern reader has to learn how to read Augustan verse in such a way that he pays sufficient, but no more than sufficient, attention to the rhyme.

[2] From Dryden's description of a 'serious play' (*Essays*, i. 100–1). His dramatic experience helped to define Dryden's conception of 'high style'. The idiom of *Annus Mirabilis*, which is modelled on *Gondibert*, is not wholly satisfactory. Later Dryden came to the conclusion that Davenant had not 'complied . . . enough *with the greatness and majesty of an heroic poem*'. (*Essays*, i. 151. My italics.) Although this refers primarily to Davenant's plays, it seems likely that Dryden was also thinking of *Gondibert*.   [3] Preface to *Religio Laici*.

one finds dignified verse which rises, as occasion offers, to that 'long majestic march, and energy divine' for which Pope gave Dryden such merited praise.

The author of one of the commendatory poems prefixed to later editions of *Absalom and Achitophel* said that Dryden

> The dialect, as well as sense, invents,
> And, with his poem, a new speech presents.[1]

What Dryden had done was to perfect a new heroic idiom. He chose his words as much for their music as their meaning: 'sounding words' is a frequent phrase throughout his criticism.[2] In his attempt to perfect the harmony of his verse he was assiduous in varying 'our old Teuton monosyllables'[3] with more 'numerous' words from the classical languages. He was helped by fifteen years' practice in the theatre—no poet has such opportunities of studying the sound of his verse as the dramatist—and by his lifelong familiarity with the music of Virgil's verse. The result was a heroic idiom of remarkable brilliance:

> Or that his Conscious Destiny made way
> By manly Beauty to Imperial Sway.[4]

The elevation of the style is most evident when a speech is to be introduced and Dryden remembers the classical poets and their modern imitators:

> Him he attempts with studied Arts to please
> And sheds his Venome in such words as these.[5]

Once or twice, as in the Miltonic description of the Temptation, the unusual arrangement of the words marks the style as heroic:

> Him Staggering so when Hells dire Agent found,
> While fainting Vertue scarce maintain'd her Ground,
> He pours fresh Forces in, and thus Replies.[6]

---

[1] Nahum Tate. S.-S. ix. 217.

[2] e.g. *Essays*, ii. 29: 'Obsolete words may then be laudably revived, when either they are more sounding, or more significant, than those in practice'; and ii. 234: 'If sounding words are not of our growth and manufacture, who shall hinder me to import them from a foreign country?' Cf. ii. 266–7.   [3] Ibid. 234.

[4] ll. 21–22.   [5] ll. 228–9.

[6] ll. 373–5. When Verrall mentions 'occasional archaisms *foreign to Dryden's own natural*

It is not suggested that the idiom of the whole poem is uniformly elevated. When such characters as Corah and Shimei are described the style is necessarily lowered. Yet it remains true that the basis of the idiom is heroic.

This can be verified by a glance at the imagery. Dryden had described 'the proper wit of an Heroic or Historical Poem' in the preface to *Annus Mirabilis*. ''Tis not the jerk or sting of an epigram, nor the seeming contradiction of a poor antithesis, . . . nor the jingle of a more poor paronomasia; neither is it so much the morality of a grave sentence; . . . but it is some lively and apt description, dressed in such colours of speech, that it sets before your eyes the absent object, as perfectly, and more delightfully than nature.'[1] In view of this passage it is not surprising to find in *Absalom and Achitophel* relatively few metaphors and similes, and practically none whose primary function is to be witty. '*Nunc non erat his locus.*'[2] Striking images occur where they are appropriate, with the object of 'amplifying' the poet's meaning or making it more emphatic. An elaborate simile

---

style, [which] point directly to the influence of the English "epics", *The Faerie Queene* and *Paradise Lost*' (p. 55, my italics), he is forgetting that decorum prescribed different idioms for poems of different 'kinds'. It is misleading to speak as if Dryden had one 'natural' style.

[1] *Essays*, i. 14–15.

[2] Ibid. 19. *The Medal*, which is written in a much 'lower' style than *Absalom*, is rich in witty imagery; for example:

> At best as little honest as he cou'd:
> And, like white Witches, mischievously good.
> To his first byass, longingly he leans;
> And *rather* would be great by wicked means.
> Thus fram'd for ill, he loos'd our Triple hold;
> (Advice unsafe, precipitous, and bold.)
> From hence those tears! that *Ilium* of our woe!
> Who helps a pow'rful Friend fore-arms a foe.
> What wonder if the Waves prevail so far,
> When He cut down the Banks that made the bar?
> Seas follow but their Nature to invade;
> But he by Art our native Strength betray'd.
> So *Sampson* to his Foe his force confest,
> And, to be shorn, lay slumb'ring on her breast.   (ll. 61–74.)

Dryden's genius never shines more brightly than when his imagination is playing round the object of his satire in this way. Images spring upwards like sparks from a glowing fire; each is allowed a moment's ascendancy, only to be followed by another. But imagery of this sort would be indecorous in a poem written in an elevated style.

is used, for example, to emphasize the effects of the plot:

> This Plot, which fail'd for want of common Sense,
> Had yet a deep and dangerous Consequence;
> For as, when raging Fevers boil the Blood
> The standing Lake soon floats into a Floud;
> And ev'ry hostile Humour which before
> Slept quiet in its Channels bubbles o're:
> So, several Factions from this first Ferment
> Work up to Foam, and threat the Government.[1]

As Dryden would have claimed, such a simile is in strict accordance with decorum. The poet has passed beyond the youthful affectation of spicing elevated verse with indecorous conceits of wit and 'settled his system of propriety'.[2] The narrative parts of the poem have a manly directness which would be spoilt by a profusion of witty images.

The relation of *Absalom and Achitophel* to heroic poetry is particularly evident in the five speeches, which may be compared with those in classical epic and *Paradise Lost*. The brilliance of these speeches as examples of forensic oratory can hardly be over-praised:[3] they are every bit as good as the celebrated 'characters'. Achitophel's first speech to Absalom is a fair representative. It begins with flattery, and passes to artful temptations to betrayal of his father. The imagery is perfectly adapted to the purposes of courtly oratory:

> Believe me, Royal Youth, thy Fruit must be
> Or gather'd Ripe, or rot upon the Tree.
> Heav'n has to all allotted, soon or late,
> Some lucky Revolution of their Fate:
> Whose Motions, if we watch and guide with Skill,
> (For humane Good depends on humane Will,)
> Our Fortune rolls as from a smooth Descent
> And, from the first impression, takes the Bent;

---

[1] ll. 134–41. The same image of the State as a patient suffering from a dangerous disease occurs in the preface: 'If the Body Politique have any Analogy to the Natural . . ., an Act of *Oblivion* were as necessary in a Hot, Distempered State, as an *Opiate* woud be in a Raging Fever.' It occurs also at ll. 756, 809–10, and 923–6.   [2] Johnson, *Lives*, i. 435.

[3] The speech from the throne is a necessary exception. It is no more dramatic than the speeches of the Miltonic Deity.

> But, if unseiz'd, she glides away like wind;
> And leaves repenting Folly far behind.
> Now, now she meets you with a glorious prize
> And spreads her Locks before her as she flies.[1]

The reminiscence of *Julius Caesar* in this speech is apt; it emphasizes that it was in the theatre that Dryden learnt the art of dramatic rhetoric. Even more brilliant are the 'few words ... but easie those and fit, More slow than Hybla drops, and far more sweet' which Absalom addresses to the crowd:

> I mourn, my Country-men, your lost Estate,
> Though far unable to prevent your Fate:
> Behold a Banish'd man, for your dear cause
> Expos'd a prey to Arbitrary Laws!
> Yet oh! that I alone coud be undone,
> Cut off from Empire, and no more a Son!
> Now all your Liberties a spoil are made;
> *Egypt* and *Tyrus* intercept your Trade,
> And *Jebusites* your Sacred Rites invade.
> My Father, whom with reverence yet I name,
> Charm'd into Ease, is careless of his Fame:
> And, brib'd with petty sums of Foreign Gold,
> Is grown in *Bathsheba*'s Embraces old:
> Exalts his Enemies, his Friends destroys,
> And all his pow'r against himself imploys.
> He gives, and let him give my right away;
> But why should he his own and yours betray?
> He onely, he can make the Nation bleed, .
> And he alone from my revenge is freed.
> Take then my tears (with that he wip'd his Eyes)
> 'Tis all the Aid my present pow'r supplies:
> No Court-Informer can these Arms accuse;
> These Arms may Sons against their Fathers use;
> And, 'tis my wish, the next Successor's reign
> May make no other *Israelite* complain.[2]

The magnificent hypocrisy of these lines is as brilliant as anything in Dryden's work; it is as skilful a use of the traditional Art of Oratory as Mark Antony's speech to the

---

[1] ll. 250–61.   [2] ll. 698–722.

Roman people. The style, as suits the speaker, the subject, and the circumstances, is simple and direct; yet each line tells like a blow on softened steel.

IV

Nothing in *Absalom and Achitophel* is more remarkable than the skill with which Dryden varies his treatment of the different characters who are introduced. It soon becomes clear how much more complex his object is than that of the mere lampooner. The measure of a man's merit or guilt, the nature of Dryden's own relations with him, his social position, and, above all, the degree of Royal favour which he enjoyed—all these considerations are taken into account before the poet determines in what way he will be treated. The presentation of Absalom, of whom there is no formal 'character', is a good example. 'The fault, on the right hand', Dryden remarks in the preface, 'is to Extenuate, Palliate, and Indulge; and, to confess freely, I have endeavoured to commit it. Besides the respect which I owe his Birth, I have a greater for his Heroick Vertues; and, *David* himself, coud not be more tender of the Young-man's Life, than I woud be of his Reputation.' As in the preface he emphasizes that 'the most excellent Natures . . . are the soonest per-verted by ill Counsels, especially when baited with Fame and Glory'[1] (it is done so suavely that we hardly notice what a remarkable case of special pleading such a contention is), so in the poem itself Dryden lays great emphasis on the

---

[1] In seeking to palliate Monmouth's conduct, Dryden remembers Milton's 'Fame is the spur' (cf. particularly ll. 297 et seq.), and makes the fullest possible use of Renaissance common-places about the 'Noble mind' being particularly subject to the temptations of Ambition:

> What cannot Praise effect in Mighty Minds,
> When Flattery Sooths and when Ambition Blinds!
> Desire of Pow'r, on Earth a Vitious Weed,
> Yet, sprung from High is of Cœlestial Seed;
> In God 'tis Glory: And when Men Aspire,
> *'Tis but a Spark too much of Heavenly Fire.*
> Th' Ambitious Youth, too Covetous of Fame,
> *Too full of Angels Metal in his Frame,*
> Unwarily was led from Vertues ways,
> Made Drunk with Honour, and debauch'd with Praise.
> ll. 303–12. (My italics.)

cunning of Achitophel, and refrains from inventing a conclusion to the story which would 'show *Absalom* Unfortunate'.[1] Not content with this, he lavishes on Absalom some of the most brilliant lines of panegyric he ever wrote.[2] He emphasizes his 'goodly person' (was he not the King's son?), and describes his reception by the crowd as 'their young *Messiah*':

> From East to West his Glories he displays:
> And, like the Sun, the Promis'd Land surveys.
> Fame runs before him as the Morning-Star,
> And shouts of Joy salute him from afar:
> Each house receives him as a Guardian God;
> And Consecrates the Place of his abode.[3]

None of the members of the King's party receives such eloquent praise. Yet in the brief characterizations of Barzillai, '*Zadoc* the Priest', 'the *Sagan* of *Jerusalem*', Adriel, Amiel, and the rest, which are examples of the *descriptio* of person expected in a heroic narrative when a new actor is introduced, a proper meed of praise is allotted to each. Although they lack the tremendous power which has immortalized the hostile 'characters', these little portraits are skilfully done.

Dryden was under personal obligations to several of the King's party, and in the passage in a more exalted style which follows the description of Barzillai (the Duke of Ormond) he repays one of his debts. In these lines, which form a brief funeral panegyric on the Duke's son, one notices the usual characteristics of the genre—exclamations,

---

[1] As Professor George R. Noyes points out in his admirable edition of Dryden (Cambridge, U.S.A., rev. ed. 1950, p. 963), ll. 957–60:

> But oh that yet he woud repent and live!
> How easie 'tis for Parents to forgive!
> With how few Tears a Pardon might be won
> From Nature, pleading for a Darling Son!

—soften the satire on Monmouth. They were added in the second edition. The same motive appears to have dictated the change of 'destroy his Prince' to 'supplant his Prince' in l. 966.

[2] In the preface to *Annus Mirabilis* Dryden remarks that 'historic and panegyric' poetry are 'branches' of 'the epic poesy' (*Essays*, i. 18). One of the main reasons for Dryden's choice of a predominantly heroic idiom for *Absalom and Achitophel* was the fact that panegyric played an important part in his plan.

[3] ll. 731–6.

sententiae, the heavenward flight of the soul, the fiction that
the poet's life has terminated with that of the dead man, and
even the circle-image beloved of Donne and his imitators, the
symbol of a perfect life:

> Oh Narrow Circle, but of Pow'r Divine,
> Scanted in Space, but perfect in thy Line![1]

In a purely satirical poem the presence of an elegiac passage
would be disconcerting. But Dryden is hardly less concerned with panegyric than with satire: he wishes to praise
the King's friends while he censures his enemies.

Like the royal party, Shaftesbury and his followers are
introduced as characters in a heroic poem. With the possible
exception of the cruel couplet about his son there is no trace
of the 'low' style in the description of Achitophel, as may
be seen by comparing it with Pope's Sporus. And there is
practically no ridicule. One has only to read the very different
'character' of Shaftesbury which Dryden wrote for *The
Medal* to see how many of the witty and sarcastic things
which might have been said about him are passed over in
silence in *Absalom and Achitophel*.[2] Dryden is intent on

[1] ll. 838–9.
[2]
> A Martial Heroe first, with early care
> Blown, like a Pigmee by the Winds, to war.
> A beardless Chief, a Rebel e'er a Man,
> (So young his hatred to his Prince began.)
> Next this, (How wildly will Ambition steer!)
> A Vermin wriggling in th' Usurper's Ear,
> Bart'ring his venal wit for sums of gold,
> He cast himself into the Saint-like mould;
> Groan'd, sigh'd, and pray'd, while Godliness was gain,
> The lowdest Bag-pipe of the Squeaking train.
> But, as 'tis hard to cheat a Juggler's Eyes,
> His open lewdness he cou'd ne'er disguise.
> There split the Saint: for Hypocritique Zeal
> Allows no Sins but those it can conceal.
> Whoring to Scandal gives too large a scope;
> Saints must not trade; but they may interlope.
> Th' ungodly Principle was all the same;
> But a gross Cheat betrays his Partner's Game.
> Besides, their pace was formal, grave, and slack;
> His nimble Wit out-ran the heavy Pack.
> Yet still he found his Fortune at a stay,
> Whole droves of Blockheads choaking up his way;

portraying Achitophel as an evil man whose existence is a perpetual threat to the safety of the State. At several points a parallel is suggested between Shaftesbury's temptation of Monmouth and the Fall of Man, with Charles himself in the background as the representative of the Deity. "Tis no more a wonder that he [Absalom] withstood not the temptations of *Achitophel*, than it was for *Adam* not to have resisted the two Devils, the Serpent and the Woman', Dryden observes in the preface. He follows the lead of a hundred Tory preachers and pamphleteers in casting Shaftesbury as 'Hells dire Agent', the Satan of the plot,

> A Name to all succeeding Ages Curst.[1]

The description of Achitophel is a reminder that satire can exist without humour.[2]

> They took, but not rewarded, his advice;
> Villain and Wit exact a double price. (ll. 26–49.)

These lines are much 'lower' than the description of Shaftesbury in *Absalom and Achitophel*. No pretence of impartiality is made: here the lines describing Shaftesbury's upright conduct as a judge would be out of place. Writing something much closer to the lampoon than *Absalom*, the poet is at liberty to be much more witty (cf. p. 62, n. 2, above).

Important as is the difference of idiom between the 'character' of Shaftesbury in *The Medal* and that in *Absalom and Achitophel*, the difference of effect is not due simply to this. In poetry, as in music, the effect is at once cumulative and complex. The force of an individual line or passage is liable to considerable modification by the context in which it appears. It is partly to this fact that we must attribute the inferiority of the 'character' of Shaftesbury in *The Medal* to that in *Absalom and Achitophel*. The plot and allegory of the latter combine with the elevated style to lend authority to the poet's judgements; while *The Medal*, brilliant as individual passages are, is too patently a lampoon to be equally effective.

[1] l. 151. In suggesting an alliance between the villain of his poem and the Devil, Dryden was following a common practice. In Milton's youthful verses *In quintum Novembris*, for example, the Devil appears to the Pope in the disguise of a venerable old man, and whispers temptations in his ear.

In the preface Dryden claims to be 'good natur'd [enough] . . . to hope with *Origen*, that the Devil himself may, at last, be sav'd'. The reference is to Achitophel.

[2] ll. 180–91 are not in the first edition. Noyes has suggested (p. 959, and cf. Macdonald, p. 21) that they were in Dryden's own manuscript, but were omitted from the first printed version 'in order to deepen the satire on Shaftesbury'.

More subtly, the *addition* of these lines may be said to enhance the effect of the satire by suggesting that the poet is being impartial. (Cf. his claim in 'To the Reader', quoted on p. 69.) They give the poem a touch of additional dignity and remove it still further from the status of a mere lampoon.

Another good reason for these lines was the fact that Shaftesbury had occupied an important judicial position to which he had been appointed by the King. If he were portrayed as an out-and-out villain, this appointment would reflect little credit on Charles. Cf. the following passage from the preface to *Naboth's Vinyard*, in which the author, who is hostile to the King,

Very different is the portrayal of the Duke of Buckingham. Whereas Achitophel is essentially a picture of an individual, and only secondly a representation of ruthless Ambition, the character of Zimri is general rather than particular: it is first of all a 'humours character' of The Inconstant Man. It also differs from the satire on Shaftesbury in its reliance on humour. Dryden's account of the matter in the *Discourse concerning . . . Satire* makes it clear that he was anxious to avoid giving mortal offence to Buckingham.[1] In this 'character', at least, he seems to have tried to make good his claim to have 'rebat[ed] the *Satyre* (where Justice would allow it), from carrying too sharp an Edge'. Yet he claims for Zimri a subtlety and indirectness which cannot be justified. The ridicule is direct. The style, inevitably, is slightly lowered, as is emphasized by the presence of two pairs of feminine rhymes.[2]

Serious scorn distinguishes the 'characters' of Shimei and Corah from that of Zimri, while an indirectness of approach involving some degree of humour marks them off even more clearly from the unsmiling arraignment of Achitophel. It is not because they are censured any less decidedly, but because commoners cannot be as dangerous to the nation as a noble-man, that there is a contemptuous humour in the lines devoted to Slingsby Bethel and Titus Oates which is completely absent from the description of Shaftesbury. The

is being ironical: 'All ingenious and ingenuous men (to whose divertisement only this Poem offers it self) will be Garrantees for the Author, that [no] Honourable and just Judge can be thought concern'd in the Character of *Arod* . . . as by the singular care and Royal goodness of his Majesty (whom God long preserve) our Benches in this Nation are furnished with persons of such eminent Integrity and Ability, that no Character of a corrupt Judge can with the least shadow of resemblance belong to them. . . .' It is just possible that Dryden's eye fell on this passage, and that he was prompted by it to temper his satire on Shaftesbury by commending his behaviour as a judge.

[1] *Essays*, ii. 93–94.

[2] The *Double Rhime* is *antiquated* grown,
   Or us'd in *Satyr* or *Burlesque* alone.

An Epistle to a Friend concerning Poetry, by Samuel Wesley (1700), ll. 575–6. Cf. Dryden, *Essays*, i. 12: 'Neither can we give ourselves the liberty of . . . using the variety of female rhymes . . . which our fathers practised' (in heroic poetry). Occasional feminine rhymes may still be found in the heroic verse of the period; but they are very frequently a sign that the style is being lowered.

'character' of Shimei begins with explicit and emphatic opprobrium:

> But he, though bad, is follow'd by a worse,
> The Wretch, who Heav'ns Anointed dar'd to Curse.

The effect of the irony which informs the whole portrait, however, modulates from pure scorn to scornful ridicule:

> *Shimei*, whose Youth did early Promise bring
> Of Zeal to God, and Hatred to his King;
> Did wisely from Expensive Sins refrain,
> And never broke the Sabbath, but for Gain . . .
> Chaste were his Cellars; and his Shrieval Board
> The Grossness of a City Feast abhor'd:
> His Cooks, with long disuse, their Trade forgot;
> Cool was his Kitchin, though his Brains were hot.[1]

The portrait of Corah, that 'Monumental Brass', is a similar compound of direct name-calling and devastating irony:

> Sunk were his Eyes, his Voice was harsh and loud,
> Sure signs he neither Cholerick was, nor Proud.[2]

It is noteworthy that such irony as may be found in the hostile 'characters' of the poem is practically always directed at religious nonconformists, whether Catholics or sectarians.[3]

V

'Besides the Writers I have mention'd,' Joseph Trapp wrote in his *Lectures on Poetry*, 'there are many others of an heroical Genius, tho' they never wrote an Heroic Poem. Among the *Latins*, *Claudian* . . . is the most eminent . . . and among those of our own Country, the late Mr. *Dryden*.'[4] Not the least interesting of the passages in which Dryden discusses his life-long aspiration to write a heroic poem occurs near the beginning of the *Discourse concerning the Original and Progress of Satire*; and it was in his long 'Varronian satire', *Absalom and Achitophel*, that he came nearest to fulfilling his ambition. It is largely to characteristics akin

---

[1] ll. 583–4, 585–8, 618–21. [2] ll. 646–7.
[3] e.g. ll. 100–7, 118–23, 128–9. [4] P. 353.

to those of heroic poetry that the poem owes its supremacy amongst the political satires in the language.[1]

Dryden's admiration for Juvenal was another reason for the idiom which he chose for his great satire. Contemporary critics contrasted the 'comical' style of Horatian satire with Juvenal's 'tragical manner'.[2] Each of the characteristics of Juvenalian satire which Dryden singles out for praise—the thoughts, 'much more elevated' than those of Horace, the 'sonorous and . . . noble' expressions, and the 'more numerous' verse[3]—proclaims its kinship with epic. It was of this dignified kind of satire that Dryden was thinking when he declared roundly that satire was undoubtedly a species of heroic poetry.[4]

The importance assigned by Renaissance critics to the moral of a heroic poem helps further to explain the relation between *Absalom and Achitophel* and heroic verse. Far from being a story told for its own sake, an epic was essentially a patriotic and didactic composition. 'The Epick Poem', said Le Bossu, 'is a discourse invented by art, to form the Manners, by such instructions as are disguised under the allegories of some one important Action, which is related in verse, after a probable, diverting and surprising manner.'[5] This description fits Dryden's poem very well.[6]

Yet the structure of *Absalom and Achitophel* has little in common with that of a heroic poem; and even for a 'historical' poem it is unsatisfactory. 'The conclusion of the Story, I purposely forbore to prosecute', Dryden remarks in the

---

[1] *Absalom and Achitophel* is more accurately described as a 'historical' than a 'heroic' poem. As the following passage from the preface to *Annus Mirabilis* makes clear, unity of action was what principally distinguished the heroic poem from the historical: 'I have called my poem *historical*, not *epic*, though both the actions and actors are as much heroic as any poem can contain. But . . . the action is not properly one, nor that accomplished in the last successes.' (*Essays*, i. 11.) I use the term 'heroic' to avoid the confusion which 'historical' brings with it.—'Historical', it may be noted, was normally used only of a poem as a whole. A historical *poem* should be written in a heroic *idiom*. Cf. *Essays*, i. 18.

[2] See below, pp. 102 et seq., and 137 et seq.

[3] *Essays*, ii. 85.

[4] Ibid. 108.

[5] *A General View of the Epick Poem*, prefixed to Pope's *Odyssey*, Sect. I, *ad fin.*

[6] And cf. Pope's remark to Spence: 'The Æneid was evidently a party piece: as much as Absalom and Achitophel' (p. 217).

preface. '. . . The Frame of it was cut out but for a Picture to the Waste; and if the Draught be so far true, 'tis as much as I design'd.'[1] Although he was not at liberty to invent a conclusion to the action, however, the chief events of the affair down to the time of writing could have been woven into a more connected narrative than the poem affords. Except in the speeches there is practically no portrayal of character in action or of the development of character and motive. The narrative parts are scamped. Whatever purpose the hemistich in the following lines is supposed to serve, for example, it gives an impression of sheer off-handedness:

> Th' inhabitants of old *Jerusalem*,
> Were *Jebusites*; the Town so call'd from them;
> And their's the Native right ——
> But when the chosen People grew more strong,
> The rightful cause at length became the wrong.[2]

Perhaps Dryden originally intended to compose a fuller narrative, and then decided that the object of his writing was gained without any further additions.

The parts of the poem not concerned with 'characters' or speeches tend rather to 'discourse', or dignified moralizing, than to narrative. *Sententiae*—'affected by Lucan, but more sparingly used by Virgil', as Dryden noted in the preface to *Annus Mirabilis*[3]—are more numerous than decorum prescribed for a heroic composition. They vary from a single line or couplet:

> But Life can never be sincerely blest:
> Heav'n punishes the bad, and proves the best[4]

---

[1] Dryden might have cited a passage from Cowley's 1656 *Preface* to justify his practice: 'It is the custom of *Heroick Poets* (as we see by the examples of *Homer* and *Virgil*, whom we should do ill to forsake to imitate others) never to come to the full end of their *Story*.' Cowley's next remark would have been too apposite: 'but onely so near [the end] that every one may see it; as men commonly play not out the game, when it is evident that they can win it, but lay down their Cards. . . .' (Spingarn, ii. 86–87).

[2] ll. 85–89. One theory about Virgil's unfinished lines was that they were meant to act as a foil to the passages which followed them, in which the poet was to exert his greatest powers. It is possible that this is the object of the half-lines in *Absalom and Achitophel*.

[3] *Essays*, i. 15.

[4] ll. 43–44. 'Sincerely'—without alloy.

through longer passages:

> So easie still it proves in Factious Times
> With publick Zeal to cancel private Crimes:
> How safe is Treason and how sacred ill,
> Where none can sin against the Peoples Will,
> Where Crouds can wink; and no offence be known,
> Since in anothers guilt they find their own[1]

to the sixty lines on Innovation,[2] which constitute a didactic passage essentially similar in rhetorical kind to many parts of *Religio Laici*.

Although the idea of the heroic poem played an important part in the conception of *Absalom and Achitophel*, it is clear that Dryden's main purpose is not narrative. His object is better indicated by the analogy with painting in the passage already quoted. The poem as a whole may be compared to a masterpiece of 'historical painting': it is written with the same purpose, that of pleasing its patron; and the canvas, which is a very large one, is crowded with figures, clearly divided into two opposing groups and painted in varying perspective. Above the head of the King hovers his 'Guardian Angel',[3] while a serpent is hinted at by the feet of Shaftesbury. Each character is brilliantly portrayed in some suitable pose, as if on a canvas by Kneller. But the whole work is more static than dynamic: action is rather implied than portrayed.

VI

What gives *Absalom and Achitophel* its characteristic tone is the blending with a heroic basis of a strong element of wit. The wit of the opening lines is one of the reasons why the heroic idiom of the poem as a whole has often been overlooked. A heroic narrative is expected to open with an invocation or some other dignified figure. *Absalom and Achitophel* opens simply; yet in a tone very different from that of *Annus*

---

[1] ll. 180–5.   [2] ll. 755–810.
[3] l. 853.

Mirabilis. Instead of the humdrum opening of the earlier poem:

> In thriving Arts long time had *Holland* grown,
> Crouching at home, and cruel when abroad:
> Scarce leaving us the means to claim our own;
> Our King they courted, and our Merchants aw'd,

Dryden wrote this:

> In pious times, e'r Priest-craft did begin,
> Before *Polygamy* was made a Sin;
> When Man on many multipli'd his kind,
> E'r one to one was cursedly confin'd . . . .

Although the idiom is not lacking in elevation, the ironical undertone is not what one expects in a heroic poem. Instead of beginning with an invocation or an exclamatory 'Fly hence' in the manner of *Naboth's Vinyard*,[1] Dryden opens his poem with a witty Saturnian setting which is reminiscent of the *Argenis* and may parody the beginning of the 'wittiest'

[1] Fly hence those *Siren*-Charms of *Wealth* and *Power*,
    Strong to undo, unable to restore.

The conclusion of *Absalom and Achitophel* also contrasts with that of *Naboth's Vinyard* (Elijah is declaring God's sentence on Achab and Jezabel):

> Thy broken Limbs, and into pieces rent,
> Shall be of Dogs the *Food* and *Excrement*:
> *Low falls thy Body*, lower thy *Soul* will sink;
> Thy Memory ever shall remain, and stink.
> And so he left them Thunder-struck and dumb;
> Stung with their present Guilt, and Fate to come.

Even the finest passage of *Naboth's Vinyard*:

> Great, and just God! will it be always so?
> When thy Rebellious Creatures here below
> Their black Designs of deepest Mischief frame,
> Shall they still *stamp* on them thy *holy Name?*
> Make thee, *All-good*, a Party in their *Ill!*
> Thy very *Word* abuse, to break thy *Will?*
> By which their *Leaders* draw the *Vulgar* in,
> With *harmless Minds*, to perpetrate their Sin;
> By which the Just are by the Impious slain,
> And *Abel* still is sacrific'd by *Cain*;
> How can thy Justice, and thy Thunder sleep,
> When such affronts on thee, and thine, they heap?
> How can the Earth forbear with open Jaws
> To swallow these Contemners of thy Laws?

—even in these lines there is an exclamatory note rare in *Absalom and Achitophel*.

of Juvenal's satires.[1] To appreciate the rhetorical triumph of the passage one must consider the difficulty with which Dryden was faced. The object of his poem was to praise the King and his party at the same time as he satirized his adversaries. The idiom he had chosen for the purpose was basically heroic. Yet it was essential to the presentation of his case to emphasize that Monmouth was the illegitimate son of the King. To have stated this in a straightforwardly elevated idiom would have been to invite ridicule. By a masterly stroke Dryden passes the matter off wittily. Instead of incontinence he attributes to the King the venerable Old Testament habit of polygamy. Enlisting anti-clerical feeling by the way, he gains his purpose with a suave audacity. Dryden once remarked that he found he had 'a soul congenial to' Chaucer's.[2] He never wrote anything more Chaucerian than the opening lines of *Absalom and Achitophel*.

'Rare poemes', Jonson tells us, 'aske rare friends',[3] and witty poems can be written only for witty patrons. Dryden was a master in the art of pleasing: *Absalom and Achitophel* was deliberately written, as every line proclaims, to please the King: and it is in the character of Charles, whose quickness in repartee and fondness for '*broad Allusions*' Halifax remarked,[4] that we find the answer to many of the questions which the poem suggests. It was because Charles was a witty man that Dryden was free to use for his poem a new alloy, a skilful blend of heroic panegyric, satire, 'discourse', and witty commentary which Lee had not dreamed of when he exhorted him to celebrate 'the troubles of majestic

---

[1] Kingesmill Long's translation of the *Argenis* begins with the words, 'The World as yet had not bowed to the Romane Scepter, nor the wide Ocean stoop't to *Tiber* . . .' (p. 1). Dryden described Juvenal's Sixth Satire (that on women) as the wittiest. His translation opens:

> In *Saturn's* Reign, at Nature's Early Birth,
> There was that Thing call'd Chastity on Earth . . .

Dryden may be insinuating that just as there was such a thing as chastity in the pagan Golden Age, so in the Golden Age of the Old Testament there was such a thing as liberty.

[2] *Essays*, ii. 265.

[3] *Epigrammes*, xciiii, l. 6.

[4] *The Complete Works of George Savile First Marquess of Halifax*, ed. Sir Walter Raleigh (1912), p. 198.

Charles'. It is the brilliant wit of *Absalom and Achitophel* that has acted as its sovereign preservative.

It is scarcely possible to exaggerate the art with which Dryden goes to work. The whole poem is a consummate example of the adaptation of means which have been perfectly mastered to the achievement of a clearly conceived end. The reader of *Absalom and Achitophel* has every opportunity of observing the benefits to verse of the close relationship maintained in the Augustan age between the Art of Oratory and the Art of Poetry.

Dryden called *Absalom and Achitophel* a satire both (by implication) in the preface to the poem and in the *Discourse concerning . . . Satire*;[1] and it is as a satire that it has always been considered. Yet it has practically nothing in common with the classical *satura*, and has marked similarities to a heroic poem. In what sense is it a satire?[2]

The answer is to be found in Luttrell's note in his copy of *Absalom and Achitophel*: 'An excellent poem agt ye Duke of Monmouth, Earl of Shaftsbury & that party & in vindication of the King & his friends.'[3] It is the prominence of the element of attack in *Absalom and Achitophel* that makes it a satire in the English sense of the word.[4]

---

[1] *Essays*, ii. 67.

[2] Verrall claimed that 'the work . . . is called by Dryden a poem and not a satire' (p. 58), thinking of the title-page. But the title-page is unlikely to have been composed by Dryden; and since he undoubtedly refers to *Absalom and Achitophel* as a satire on two occasions, very little significance can be attached to this.

[3] Quoted by Macdonald, p. 20.

[4] In my attempt to emphasize the wit of *Absalom and Achitophel* I am particularly indebted to Miss Helen Gardner.

A COMPLEX MOCK-HEROIC:
THE RAPE OF THE LOCK

If the Moderns have excelled the Ancients in any species of writing,
it seems to be in satire: and, particularly in that kind of satire, which
is conveyed in the form of the epopee. . . . As the poet disappears in
this way of writing, and does not deliver the intended censure in his
own proper person, the satire becomes more delicate, because more
oblique. Add to this, that a tale or story more strongly engages and
interests the reader, than a series of precepts or reproofs, or even of
characters themselves, however lively and natural. An heroi-comic
poem may therefore be justly esteemed the most excellent kind of
satire.

JOSEPH WARTON[1]

'THE first principle of Criticism', Pope wrote in the postscript to his translation of the *Odyssey*, 'is to consider the nature of the piece, and the intent of its author.'[2] In *The Rape of the Lock* neither is in doubt. The incident on which the poem is founded had caused a breach between the two families of the Petres and the Fermors, and it was suggested to Pope that he should help 'to make a jest of it, and laugh them together again'.[3]

The writing of a witty narrative poem was one of the most obvious methods; and no species of narrative was more eligible than the mock-heroic, so highly praised by Dryden.[4] It was a genre which had much to recommend it. It had been evolved for the very purpose of 'diminishing' petty quarrels, and combined the two sorts of writing in which the age was most interested: epic and satire. And there was still a spice of novelty about it. Rowe had even questioned 'if it can be call'd a Kind, that is so new in the World, and of which we have had so few Instances'.[5] While *Le Lutrin* and

---

[1] *An Essay on the Genius and Writings of Pope. In Two Volumes* (4th ed., 1782), i. 211.
[2] Para. 1.   [3] Spence, p. 194.   [4] See pp. 44–45 above.
[5] *Boileau's Lutrin: A Mock-Heroic Poem . . . Render'd into English Verse* [by J. OZELL]. *To which is prefix'd some Account of Boileau's Writings, and this Translation. By N. Rowe Esq . . . 1708*, p. [A5r].

The Dispensary (whose composition Pope had followed with keen interest) were suitable models, neither of them was so brilliant as to be discouraging. Pope may well have aspired to write a consummate example of the mock-heroic genre before Lord Petre stole the lock: it may be that in the quarrel of the Petres and the Fermors he merely found matter and opportunity for the attempt.

While modern critics often think of a mock-heroic poem primarily as a satire on the epic,[1] the Augustans laid the emphasis elsewhere. The technical brilliance of *The Rape of the Lock* is largely due to the care with which Pope had studied the great epics and the remarks of the critics with a view to writing an epic of his own. Nor did the success of his mock-epic make a heroic poem seem a less worthy ambition; for he was planning an epic until the last days of his life.[2]

The writers who did ridicule the epic in the Augustan age were the authors of burlesques and travesties; and Dennis was not alone in thinking their object 'a very scurvy one'.[3] In mock-epic a dignified genre is turned to witty use without being cheapened in any way. The poet has an opportunity of ridiculing through incongruity, and of affording his reader the sophisticated pleasure of recognizing ironical parallels to familiar passages in Homer and Virgil. A mock-heroic poem is a 'parody' of the epic, but a parody in the Augustan sense, not in the modern.[4] The 'new purpose' of the frequent 'allusions' throughout *The Rape of the Lock* is not the ridicule of a literary form but the setting of a lovers' tiff in true perspective.

---

[1] 'The most rudimentary requisite of a mock-heroic poem is, that it should mock the epic.' Courthope, *E.-C.* v. 97.

[2] See Edward Young's 'Conjectures on Original Composition' (*Works*, 1774, vi. 93). Cf. Spence, quoted on p. 5, above.

See Addison's remark, near the end of his 'Essay on the *Georgics*', that 'the last *Georgic* was a good Prelude to the *Æneis*; and very well shew'd what the Poet could do in the description of what was really great, by his describing the Mock-grandeur of an Insect with so good a grace . . .'

[3] Preface to *Miscellanies in Verse and Prose* (1693). Hooker, i. 8.

[4] See above, p. 51.

II

The fact that the 1712 version of *The Rape of the Lock*
consists of no more than 334 lines and takes over only a few
of the characteristics of the epic makes it clear that Pope's
concern was less with Homer and Virgil than with Miss
Fermor and Lord Petre. The style is heroic; but the invocation, the proposition of the subject, the descriptions, the
moralizing asides, the speeches and the battle are practically
the only structural features modelled on the epic. Clearly the
poet's purpose at this stage was neither to ridicule the heroic
genre nor to provide a humorous parallel to all the principal
ingredients of epic, but to 'diminish' the affair of the lock of
hair. This remains true in the 1714 version, in which Pope
increased the length of the poem from two cantos to five
(totalling 794 lines) and added such further 'allusions' to the
epic as the visit to the Cave of Spleen (parodying the epic
visit to the underworld), the game of ombre (parodying the
heroic games), the adorning of Belinda (which parallels the
arming of Achilles), and above all the extensive 'machinery'
of Ariel and the sylphs.[1]

That Pope should have considered the addition of further
machinery is not surprising. Le Bossu had said that 'the
Machinery crowns the whole work',[2] while Dryden drew
the conclusion that 'no heroic poem can be writ on the
Epicurean [i.e. atheistical] principles'.[3] Pope was conversant
with the formidable mass of criticism in which the function
and nature of epic machinery had been discussed from the
early days of the Renaissance onwards, and must have given
a great deal of thought to the matter as he worked on his
never-abandoned plans for an epic of his own.

In the early version of the poem Pope compromised.
While supernatural agents play practically no part in the
action, Lord Petre prays to Love and Jove's scales decide

---

[1] All quotations in this chapter are from the 1714 text as edited by Geoffrey Tillotson in
vol. ii of the Twickenham edition (1940).

[2] *A General View of the Epick Poem . . . Extracted from Bossu*, and prefixed to Pope's
Odyssey. Sect. VII.   [3] *Essays*, ii. 210.

the issue of the battle between the beaux and belles, while
the Muse, Sol, Phoebus, 'Pow'rs', Winds, 'the just Gods',
Time and Fate, Cupid's flames, and 'Heav'n' are all mentioned.[1] Yet they are little more than rhetorical 'heightening',
figures of speech used to lend emphasis at important points
in the action. If a more extended parody of the epic was to
be attempted, machinery of a more striking sort had to be
found.

One possibility would have been to revive the classical
deities, peopling the Mall and Hampton Court with Pan
and all his quality: another to have followed Boileau in
setting personified moral qualities to preside over the action
of the poem. But Pope shared Johnson's dislike of old
mythology in modern poetry, and knew as well as he that
'we should have turned away from a contest between Venus
and Diana';[2] while the fact that the visit to the Cave of
Spleen is the least delightful part of the poem suggests that
Pope did well to decline to follow any farther the example
of Boileau. It was not by modelling his machinery on Discord, Piety, and Faith and the other cold personifications of
Le Lutrin that Pope was to make The Rape of the Lock the
subtle masterpiece of its kind.

By a stroke of luck and of genius Pope hit on the notion
of basing his machinery on the Rosicrucian spirits recently
described in Le Comte de Gabalis.[3] Once the idea occurred
to him every thought he gave to the matter must have made
the choice seem the more fortunate. Since Bayle had described the Rosicrucians as 'but a Sect of Mountebanks',[4]

---

[1] I owe the point that the sylphs are not the only 'machinery' in the poem to Professor
Tillotson (Twickenham ed., ii. pp. 121–2).   [2] Lives, iii. 233.

[3] In the French editions of 1670 and 1700 and the English translations of Philip Ayres and
A. Lovell (both 1680) this work was fairly well known. (See Tillotson, Twickenham ed., ii.
356–61.) Pope tells Miss Fermor in his Dedication that 'many of the Fair Sex have read it
. . . by Mistake [for a Novel]'. Pope's attention may have been drawn to it by a reference to
the Rosicrucians in the Spectator for 15 May 1712, which appeared between the completion of the first version of The Rape of the Lock and the time when he began to augment it.

[4] The Diverting History of the Count de Gabalis . . . To which is prefix'd, Monsieur Bayle's
Account of this Work, and of the Sect of the Rosicrucians . . . The Second Edition. London . . .
1714, p. [A4r]. As the title suggests, the book was written purely to 'divert'. The narrator
regards the Count as an amusing madman.

the creatures in whom they believed had about them a suggestion of the fanciful and the far-fetched which made them
particularly suitable for a mock-epic. Great scope for description was given by the fact that the Rosicrucians identified
their sylphs, gnomes, nymphs, and salamanders at once
with the pagan deities and (with a fine catholicism) with the
'Gothic' fairies of the Middle Ages.[1] Their 'Elementary
Nations'[2] combined the mischievous habits of the latter with
the interest in human life characteristic of Venus and Diana.
They delight—the Count tells his interlocutor—'in teaching
[human beings] to live morally; [and] in giving them most
wise and salutary Counsels'.[3] This enabled Pope to parody,
inter alia, the use of 'Guardian Angels' in heroic verse recommended by Dryden and practised by Cowley.[4]

Even more important was the erotic quality of the Rosicrucian spirits. Le Bossu pointed out that 'each Epick Poem
has . . . some peculiar *Passion*, which distinguishes it in
particular from other Epick Poems, and constitutes a kind
of singular and individual difference between these Poems
of the same Species. These singular Passions correspond to
the *Character* of the *Hero*.'[5] It is not surprising that as the
'peculiar Passions' of the *Iliad* are '*Anger* and *Terrour* . . .
because *Achilles* is angry, and the most Terrible of all Men',
while 'the *soft* and *tender Passions*' reign in the *Æneid*,
'because that is the Character of *Æneas*', so coquetry is the
reigning passion in Pope's epic of Belinda's stolen lock.[6] The
erotic interest of *Le Comte de Gabalis* is very marked. The
principal object of the Rosicrucian spirits is to carry on

---

[1] pp. 25 and 86.　　　　　　　[2] p. 45.　　　　　　　[3] pp. 45-46.
[4] Cf., in particular, *R.L.* ii. 87-90:

> Others on Earth o'er human Race preside,
> Watch all their Ways, and all their Actions guide:
> Of these the Chief the Care of Nations own,
> And guard with Arms Divine the *British Throne*,

with Dryden's *Essays*, ii. 34: 'There are guardian angels, appointed by God Almighty, as
his vicegerents, for the protection and government of cities, provinces, kingdoms, and
monarchies. . . .'

[5] Sect. VI.

[6] Pride is also prominent (see pp. 94-95 below); but pride and coquetry are not un-
connected.

love-affairs with human beings, because in this way they are permitted to gain immortality. Initiates of the cult renounce mortal women[1] and take as their mistresses nymphs and sylphs, whose 'Beauty is exquisite, and incomparably beyond that of the Daughters of Men'.[2] Piquancy is added by the fact that the Rosicrucian spirits, jealous as they are of mortal women, do not restrict their lovers to one member of their own elemental race.

While Pope found in the Rosicrucian doctrine many hints which he could develop, however, the supernatural agents of *The Rape of the Lock* are essentially his own creation. The Rosicrucians held that spirits could change their sex at will;[3] but the main emphasis throughout *Le Comte de Gabalis* is laid on their attractions for men as 'elementary' mistresses. In Pope's poem, on the other hand, they figure primarily as the allies of women in their unceasing war with men.[4] Nor did Pope find in *de Gabalis* more than the slightest hints towards the airy beauty of his supernatural beings. The main thing that he took over was merely the licence to invent a fantastic race whose presence would make every trivial incident in his poem 'appear of the utmost Importance'.[5] The sylphs are mirrors added to his scene. By them the central action is reflected and multiplied a hundredfold,

---

[1] Pope adapts the idea, and makes Ariel retire from Belinda 'amaz'd, confus'd' when she sees

An Earthly Lover lurking at her Heart. (iii. 143–6.)

[2] p. 14.

[3] p. 64. Cf. *R.L.* i. 69–70.

[4] When she wishes to impress on Belinda the fact of imminent danger, however, Ariel makes use of her ability to assume the male sex. This example of 'propriety' may be illustrated by a note by Eustathius which Brome cited in Pope's *Odyssey* (vi. 24 n.): 'The judgment with which [Homer] introduces the vision is remarkable: in the *Iliad*, when he is to give an air of importance to his vision, he clothes it in the likeness of *Nestor*, the wisest person of the Army.... Here the Poet sends a vision to a young Lady, under the resemblance of a young Lady: he adapts the circumstances to the person, and describes the whole with an agreeable propriety.' Pope, too, 'adapts the circumstances to the person', suggesting that there are messengers to whom a young lady like Belinda is more likely to pay attention than another young lady—such as 'a *Birth-night Beau*'.

Pope may also be recalling Dryden's remark, in *The Author's Apology for Heroic Poetry and Poetic Licence*, that Scripture itself 'accommodates itself to vulgar apprehension, in giving angels the likeness of beautiful young men'. (*Essays*, i. 187.)

[5] Dedication.

gaining in subtlety and mystery as well as in ironical importance.[1]

III

The creation of the sylphs allowed Pope's imagination a much wider scope than before. 'An heroic poet is not tied to a bare representation of what is true, or exceedingly probable', Dryden had written; '. . . he may let himself loose to visionary objects, and to the representation of such things as depending not on sense, and therefore not to be comprehended by knowledge, may give him a freer scope for imagination.'[2] The epic poet's task of arousing 'admiration' was particularly associated with the supernatural machinery of his poem.[3] In the description of the sylphs and their actions Pope made his own bid to arouse 'admiration'.

English poetry contains no passage of description more exquisite than that of the sylphs in Canto II of *The Rape of the Lock*.

Of the four 'Elementary Nations' Pope concentrates on the sylphs, whose region is the air; and air is the element which informs every line of his description:

> He summons strait his Denizens of Air;
> The lucid Squadrons round the Sails repair:
> Soft o'er the Shrouds Aerial Whispers breathe,
> That seem'd but *Zephyrs* to the Train beneath.
> Some to the Sun their Insect-Wings unfold,
> Waft on the Breeze, or sink in Clouds of Gold.

---

[1] One of the least frivolous of the objections which Dennis made to the machinery of *The Rape of the Lock* was that it 'do[es] not in the least influence [the] Action'. (*Remarks on Mr. Pope's Rape of the Lock*, Letter IV; Hooker, ii. 337.) Pope might have defended himself by citing Le Bossu's distinction between machines which require '*Human Probability*' and those to which '*Divine Probability*' only is proper. (Sect. VII.) The latter class, he rules, 'should be so disengaged from the Action, that one might subtract them from it, without destroying the Action'. The sylphs appear to conform precisely to the requirements of the class of machines to which '*Divine Probability*' only is appropriate.

[2] *Essays*, i. 153.

[3] 'Without *admiration*', Richard Hurd wrote as late as 1762, '(which cannot be effected but by the marvellous of celestial intervention, I mean, the agency of superior natures really existing, or by the illusion of the fancy taken to be so) no epic poem can be long lived.' *Letters on Chivalry and Romance*, ed. Edith J. Morley (1911), p. 144. On the earlier history of the term see G. Gregory Smith, *Elizabethan Critical Essays* (1904), i. 392–3.

> Transparent Forms, too fine for mortal Sight,
> Their fluid Bodies half dissolv'd in Light.
> Loose to the Wind their airy Garments flew,
> Thin glitt'ring Textures of the filmy Dew.[1]

After the aetherial beauty of these lines Pope takes up the slightest of hints in *Le Comte de Gabalis* and describes some of the colours which the sylphs display:

> Dipt in the richest Tincture of the Skies,
> Where Light disports in ever-mingling Dies,
> While ev'ry Beam new transient Colours flings,
> Colours that change whene'er they wave their Wings.
> Amid the Circle, on the gilded Mast,
> Superior by the Head, was *Ariel* plac'd;
> His Purple Pinions opening to the Sun,
> He rais'd his Azure Wand, and thus begun.[2]

Such colour is only one aspect of the beauty which Pope describes. Throughout the poem the senses are flattered as delicately as they are in Belinda's world itself. It is fitting that the punishments inflicted on negligent sylphs should be the quintessence of torture of the senses. Such a sinner

> Shall feel sharp Vengeance soon o'ertake his Sins,
> Be stopt in *Vials*, or transfixt with *Pins*;
> Or plung'd in Lakes of bitter *Washes* lie,
> Or wedg'd whole Ages in a *Bodkin's* Eye:
> *Gums* and *Pomatums* shall his Flight restrain,
> While clog'd he beats his silken Wings in vain;
> Or Alom-*Stypticks* with contracting Power
> Shrink his thin Essence like a rivell'd Flower.[3]

While the machinery gave Pope an unrivalled opportunity of indulging his descriptive powers, the descriptive passages in *The Rape of the Lock* are by no means confined to those

---

[1] ii. 55–64.   [2] ii. 65–72.

[3] ii. 125–32. Part of the amusement offered to the reader of a mock-heroic poem is to see all the objects familiar in some particular milieu skilfully introduced. So Boileau described the trappings of a church, and Garth those of a dispensary. Neither displayed the skill shown in *The Rape of the Lock*. The words italicized in the original edition (and so printed by the Twickenham editor) are those which Pope took pride in introducing from 'the female world'. Italics are used throughout the poem for the same purpose (as well as to indicate proper names).

dealing with the sylphs and their elemental colleagues. Perhaps it is because a mock-heroic poem has been thought of primarily as a satire on epic that the immense difference made by the nature of the poet's subject has often been over-looked. *Le Lutrin*, *The Dispensary*, and *The Rape of the Lock* are all mock-heroic poems describing a quarrel; but while Boileau and Garth describe the quarrels of lazy priests and grubby physicians, Pope is concerned with a quarrel in the *beau monde*. The nature of Pope's subject (and of his inten-tion) leads to an immense difference between his 'mock-epic' and those of Boileau and Garth.

Whereas the descriptions in *Le Lutrin* and *The Dispensary* (to which *MacFlecknoe* may be added) are characteristically of 'low' scenes, a fat priest asleep or the building of a dis-pensary in the poorest quarter of London,[1] the background of *The Rape of the Lock* is a brilliant one. In lines already quoted Dryden had parodied the *descriptio* of the heroic poem in this way:

> Close to the Walls which fair *Augusta* bind,
> (The fair *Augusta* much to fears inclin'd)
> An ancient fabrick rais'd t'inform the sight,
> There stood of yore, and *Barbican* it hight:
> A watch Tower once, but now, so Fate ordains,
> Of all the Pile an empty name remains.
> From its old Ruins Brothel-houses rise,
> Scenes of lewd loves, and of polluted joys. . . .[2]

Very different is the scene which Pope describes:

> Close by those Meads for ever crown'd with Flow'rs,
> Where *Thames* with Pride surveys his rising Tow'rs,
> There stands a Structure of Majestick Frame,
> Which from the neighb'ring *Hampton* takes its Name.[3]

The descriptions in *The Rape of the Lock* are 'mock-heroic' in a very different sense from those in *MacFlecknoe* and *The*

---

[1] Garth felt the need to escape from the close atmosphere of *The Dispensary* (which has a good deal in common with that of the *Dunciad*), and did so by including a number of passages of picturesque natural description, such as that of the Fortunate Isles. But these stand out as excrescences.

[2] *MacFlecknoe*, ll. 64–71.   [3] iii. 1–4.

Dispensary. Whereas Dryden and Garth had described ugly things with ironical elevation of style, Pope had objects of great beauty to describe. His poem is shot through with strands of silk from the fashionable world.

I V

'If Virgil has merited such perpetual commendation for exalting his bees, by the majesty and magnificence of his diction', wrote Joseph Warton in his *Essay*, 'does not POPE deserve equal praises, for the pomp and lustre of his language, on so trivial a subject?'[1] The 'pomp and lustre' of the idiom in which *The Rape of the Lock* is written is evident from the opening lines onwards:

> What dire Offence from am'rous Causes springs,
> What mighty Contests rise from trivial Things,
> I sing . . .

One notes the inversion of the order of the words, the epithets, the use of the relatively 'pompous' word 'Contests' (earlier Pope had written 'Quarrels'[2]), and the dignified march of the verse.[3] A similar elevation is particularly noticeable at the end of Canto III:

> What Time wou'd spare, from Steel receives its date,
> And Monuments, like Men, submit to Fate!
> Steel cou'd the Labour of the Gods destroy,
> And strike to Dust th'Imperial Tow'rs of *Troy*;
> Steel cou'd the Works of mortal Pride confound,
> And hew Triumphal Arches to the Ground.
> What wonder then, fair Nymph! thy Hairs shou'd feel
> The conq'ring Force of unresisted Steel?

One has only to glance into the *Homer* to find a serious use of what is basically the same style:

> Refresh'd, they wait them to the bow'r of state,
> Where circled with his Peers *Atrides* sat:

---

[1] i. 239.   [2] Twickenham ed., ii. 144.
[3] Contrast the colloquial opening of the *Epistle to Arbuthnot*:

> Shut, shut the door, good *John!* . . .

As the latter part of that line reminds us ('fatigu'd I said'), inversions do occur in poems of the lower kinds. But in *R.L.* they are much more numerous; e.g. i. 11–12, 25, 47, 113.

> Thron'd next the King, a fair attendant brings
> The purest product of the crystal springs;
> High on a massy vase of silver mold,
> The burnish'd laver flames with solid gold:
> In solid gold the purple vintage flows,
> And on the board a second banquet rose.[1]

The similarity of idiom between *The Rape of the Lock* and the *Homer* is nowhere more obvious than in the descriptions of the battles between the *beaux* and *belles* and between the opposing cards in the game of ombre:

> Now move to War her Sable *Matadores*,
> In Show like Leaders of the swarthy *Moors*. . . .[2]

It is because the idiom of Pope's mock-epic differs from that of epic itself only in being more brilliant and (in an honourable sense) more 'laboured' that he was able to work into the texture of his verse such numerous and successful parodies of the classical epics.

Even a heroic poem, however, was not expected to maintain the same elevation throughout. If bombast is to be avoided 'the diction is to follow the images,[3] and to take its colour from the complexion of the thoughts. Accordingly the *Odyssey* is not always cloathed in the majesty of verse proper to Tragedy, but sometimes descends into the plainer Narrative, and sometimes even to that familiar dialogue essential to Comedy.'[4] Of several passages in *The Rape of the Lock* where the style is noticeably lowered, the most obvious is the description of Sir Plume:

> (Sir *Plume*, of *Amber Snuff-box* justly vain,
> And the nice Conduct of a *clouded Cane*)
> With earnest Eyes, and round unthinking Face,
> He first the Snuff-box open'd, then the Case,
> And thus broke out—'My Lord, why, what the Devil?
> 'Z—ds! damn the Lock! 'fore Gad, you must be civil!
> 'Plague on't! 'tis past a Jest—nay prithee, Pox!
> 'Give her the Hair'—he spoke, and rapp'd his Box.[5]

---

[1] *Odyssey*, iv. 61–68.   [2] iii. 47–48.
[3] Here, the objects or actions which the poet describes.
[4] Postscript to the *Odyssey*, para. xvi.   [5] iv. 123–30.

These lines remind us, by contrast, of the absence from the rest of the poem of the direct satiric 'characters' so frequent in Pope's other work. In this one passage Pope lowers his style to what Gildon called 'something New; Heroic Doggrel . . . but lately found out, where the Verse and the Subject agree'.[1]

But many of the speeches are among the most elevated passages in *The Rape of the Lock*. Pope told a friend that he was sketching an essay on the Oratory of Homer and Virgil;[2] and one of the 'very laborious and uncommon sort of indexes' which he appended to his translation of the *Iliad* shows the seriousness with which he regarded the ancient poets as rhetorical models. It divides Homer's speeches into classes, the Exhortatory or Deliberative, the Vituperative, the Narrative, the Pathetic, and the Sarcastic. Examples of each class are readily found in *The Rape of the Lock*.

The cumulative figures so prominent in the speeches are only one instance of the occurrence throughout *The Rape of the Lock* of the dignified 'colours of rhetoric' associated with the heroic poem. In a note on the *Odyssey*, Pope observed that 'sentences are not only allowable, but beautiful in Heroick Poetry, if they are introduced with propriety and without affectation'.[3] There are several instances in *The Rape of the Lock*:

> Oh thoughtless Mortals! ever blind to Fate,
> Too soon dejected, and too soon elate!
> Sudden these Honours shall be snatch'd away,
> And curs'd for ever this Victorious Day.[4]

Such *sententiae*, which are introduced at points where there is a structural demand for increased elevation and solemnity,

---

[1] *The New Rehearsal, or Bays the Younger* (1714), pp. 42–43. Quoted in Bond, *English Burlesque Poetry 1700–1750*, pp. 75–76. There can be little doubt that the lines on 'Sir Plume', unlike by far the greater part of *The Rape of the Lock*, were animated by personal dislike. Pope's caricature was acknowledged 'the very picture of the man' (Spence, p. 195). There is something disingenuous in the feigned surprise with which Pope wrote to a friend: 'Sir Plume blusters, I hear' (*E.-C.* vi. 162). He was far too conscious an artist to be unaware that his lines would hurt. What was the nature of the grudge he bore Sir George Browne? Other passages rather 'low' for the general level of the poem are iv. 49–54 and v. 115–22.

[2] *E.-C.* ix. 71.   [3] VII. 379 n.   [4] iii. 101–4.

wittily emphasize the poet's 'high seriousness' and serve (at the same time) as remarkably effective transitions. The lines which follow the description of the mischievous effect of coffee on Lord Petre, for example, do not only parody *Absalom and Achitophel*: they also serve as a hinge between that paragraph and the one which follows:

> Ah cease rash Youth! desist ere 'tis too late,
> Fear the just Gods, and think of *Scylla*'s Fate!
> Chang'd to a Bird, and sent to flit in Air,
> She dearly pays for *Nisus*' injur'd Hair!
> *But when to Mischief Mortals bend their Will,*
> *How soon they find fit Instruments of Ill!*
> Just then, *Clarissa* drew with tempting Grace
> A two-edg'd Weapon from her shining Case. . . .[1]

If Pope was right when he said that 'the use of pompous expression for low actions . . . is . . . the perfection of the Mock Epick',[2] *The Rape of the Lock* passes the test with the highest honours. Periphrasis, for example, which is one of the manifestations of 'eighteenth-century poetic diction' which has most frequently been attacked, is skilfully employed. In his translation of *Le Lutrin* Ozell had playfully elaborated Boileau's direct reference[3] into a jocose periphrastic description of the things 'in Vulgar Speech call'd NAILS'. In the same spirit Pope uses 'many periphrases, and uncommon appellations'[4] for the scissors with which Lord Petre performs the rape—'two-edg'd Weapon', 'little Engine', 'glitt'ring *Forfex*', 'fatal Engine', 'Sheers', and 'meeting Points'.

At no point in *The Rape of the Lock* are epic methods of 'heightening' merely reproduced, any more than they are merely ridiculed: they are always subtly adapted to Pope's

---

[1] iii. 121–8. (My italics.) Cf. *Absalom and Achitophel*, ll. 79 et seq. And see Spence's remark that in the best poets the 'Sentences are so far from hindering the Narration, that they are almost constantly a part of it, and help to carry it forward'. (*An Essay on Pope's Odyssey* (Part II, 1727), p. 269.) I find that Professor Tillotson has already drawn attention to the skilful transitions in this part of the poem (*On the Poetry of Pope* (second edition, 1950), pp. 49–51).   [2] Postscript to the *Odyssey*, para. xxiii.

[3] Boileau says simply 'de longs clous il prend une poignée' (ii. 85)..

[4] Warton, i. 243 n.

own ends. This may be seen in the vaunting oath sworn by
Lord Petre:

> While Fish in Streams, or Birds delight in Air,
> Or in a Coach and Six the *British* Fair,
> As long as *Atalantis* shall be read,
> Or the small Pillow grace a Lady's Bed,
> While *Visits* shall be paid on solemn Days,
> When numerous Wax-lights in bright Order blaze,
> While Nymphs take Treats, or Assignations give,
> So long my Honour, Name, and Praise shall live![1]

Pope is here using the classical formula, with a witty
appropriateness, to fill in the picture of Belinda's world. The
carefully selected details emphasize the artificiality of the
milieu which he describes. Similarly the yoking together of
ideas which normally belong to very different levels of
seriousness has a strongly satirical effect:

> Sooner shall Grass in *Hide*-Park *Circus* grow,
> And Wits take Lodgings in the Sound of *Bow*;
> Sooner let Earth, Air, Sea, to *Chaos* fall,
> Men, Monkies, Lap-dogs, Parrots, perish all![2]

Just as it is uncertain what disaster is imminent in Canto II—

> Whether the Nymph shall break *Diana*'s Law,
> Or some frail *China* Jar receive a Flaw,
> Or stain her Honour, or her new Brocade[3]

(an effect concisely obtained by zeugma in the line 'Or lose
her Heart, or Necklace, at a Ball'[4])—so

> Not youthful Kings in Battel seiz'd alive,
> Not scornful Virgins who their Charms survive,
> Not ardent Lovers robb'd of all their Bliss,
> Not ancient Ladies when refus'd a Kiss,
> Not Tyrants fierce that unrepenting die,
> Not *Cynthia* when her *Manteau*'s pinn'd awry,
> E'er felt such Rage, Resentment and Despair,
> As Thou, sad Virgin! for thy ravish'd Hair![5]

---

[1] iii. 163–70.

[2] iv. 117–20.

[3] ii. 105–7. Cf. iii. 13–14.

[4] ii. 109.

[5] iv. 3–10. Cf. iii. 157–60.

Such passages, like the single line

> Puffs, Powders, Patches, Bibles, Billet-doux,[1]

emphasize the topsy-turvy chaos of values in Belinda's world. It is the same fragile universe as that in the *Verses on the Death of Dr. Swift*, painted with more forbearance.

V

Unlike *MacFlecknoe*, *The Rape of the Lock* contains very few of the directly 'diminishing' images of straightforward satire.[2] Far more numerous are mock-heroic images which enhance the effect of the fundamental irony.

> Not fierce *Othello* in so loud a Strain
> Roar'd for the Handkerchief that caus'd his Pain[3]

as Belinda called for the ravished lock.

> [As] Ladies in Romance assist their Knight,
> Present the Spear, and arm him for the Fight,[4]

so Clarissa hands the fatal scissors to Lord Petre. The apotheosis of the lock is illustrated from Roman myth:

> So *Rome*'s great Founder to the Heav'ns withdrew,
> To *Proculus* alone confess'd in view.[5]

The game of ombre is dignified by several elaborate similes (notably that which compares the scattering of the cards to the dispersal of a 'routed Army'),[6] as is the battle of the *beaux* and *belles*:

> So when bold *Homer* makes the Gods engage,
> And heav'nly Breasts with human Passions rage;
> 'Gainst *Pallas*, *Mars*; *Latona*, *Hermes* Arms;
> And all *Olympus* rings with loud Alarms.
> *Jove*'s Thunder roars, Heav'n trembles all around;
> Blue *Neptune* storms, the bellowing Deeps resound:
> *Earth* shakes her nodding Tow'rs, the Ground gives way;
> And the pale Ghosts start at the Flash of Day![7]

'A game of romps was never so well dignified before.'[8]

---

[1] i. 138.

[2] Examples, however, may be found at i. 100 and iv. 54. For such imagery in *MacFlecknoe* see pp. 48–49 above.   [3] v. 105–6.   [4] iii. 129–30.   [5] v. 125–6.

[6] iii. 81–86.   [7] v. 45–52.   [8] Warton, i. 248.

Such are the images which one expects to find in a mock-heroic poem. Less simple in its effect is the comparison of Belinda to the sun at the beginning of Canto II:

> Not with more Glories, in th'Etherial Plain,
> The Sun first rises o'er the purpled Main,
> Than issuing forth, the Rival of his Beams
> Launch'd on the Bosom of the Silver *Thames.*

There is a paradox about this image which is the paradox about the whole poem. In the simple mock-heroic, of which *MacFlecknoe* is a good example, the subject of the poem is compared to something great and made ridiculous by the comparison. It is 'a sort of [deliberate] transgression against the rules of proportion and mechanicks: it is using a vast force to lift a *feather*'.[1] The comparison of Shadwell to Hannibal is, simply, comic; and the result is denigration. The comparison of Belinda to the sun is different. It is a wild exaggeration, hardly less absurd for being a commonplace image in love poetry; and Pope was fully aware of its absurdity. But it is not merely absurd: it contains an element of the same imaginative truth as the line

> *Belinda* smil'd, and all the World was gay.[2]

What is true of the comparison of Belinda to the sun is true of the whole conception of *The Rape of the Lock*. There is an element of the incongruous in comparing a pretty girl to the sun and describing her life in the style appropriate to the adventures of a hero, but it is a different incongruity from that created by comparing Shadwell to Hannibal and describing his 'coronation' in the heroic style. While the heroic idiom of *MacFlecknoe* merely ridicules, the heroic idiom of *The Rape of the Lock* has its measure of appropriateness as well as of inappropriateness. Eighteenth-century theorists referred to the 'dignity' with which the mock-heroic treatment of a trivial subject invests it: whereas in

---

[1] I have adapted a sentence from para. xxi of the Postscript to the *Odyssey.*
[2] ii. 52.

MacFlecknoe this dignity is wholly ironical, in *The Rape of the Lock* it is not.

MacFlecknoe is a poem against Shadwell, a lampoon making no pretensions to a moral purpose: *The Rape of the Lock* is not a poem against anyone. In so far as it is a satire, it opposes not a person but a moral fault: immoderate female pride. Its satire is not directed against Arabella Fermor but against a weakness which she shares with half the world. There is a further difference. While every line in *MacFlecknoe* contributes to the annihilation of Shadwell, it is not true that every line in *The Rape of the Lock* directly satirizes women's folly. Pope's object is quite different from Dryden's. Dryden wished to laugh Shadwell out of court. Pope wishes to laugh the quarrel out of court, and in such a way as to give serious offence to nobody.[1] Dryden's aim is to arouse in the reader's mind contempt for Shadwell: Pope's is to conciliate everybody by means of mirth.

This peculiarity in the tone of *The Rape of the Lock* was noticed by Dennis. 'What can this Author mean', he asks angrily, 'by creating in his Readers an Expectation of Pleasantry [by describing his poem as *Heroi-Comical*], when there is not so much as one Jest in his Book?'[2] What annoyed him (apart from personal dislike of Pope) was that the reader of *The Rape of the Lock* is seldom encouraged to throw back his head and laugh. Dennis looked for the comedy of absurd incidents exemplified by *Hudibras* and *MacFlecknoe*.[3] Pope supplied comedy of a different sort—a subtler irony akin to the high comedy of Molière.

VI

The moral of *The Rape of the Lock* must not be forgotten. If he meant to include the poem amongst the early work in which 'pure Description held the Place of Sense',[4] Pope was

---

[1] Except—I conjecture—Sir George Browne: see p. 88, n. 1, above.
[2] *Remarks*, Letter I (Hooker, ii. 328).
[3] Ibid., Letter II (Hooker, ii. 331).
[4] *Epistle to Dr. Arbuthnot*, l. 148.

being deliberately unfair. *The Rape of the Lock* is itself the best evidence that 'Sense' may be expressed by means of a 'fable' and made more vivid by narrative and description. For all his delight in the beauty of Belinda's world Pope never allows it to arrogate the place which rightly belongs to the sovereignty of Sense.

The full complexity of his attitude may be examined in the lines in which 'Belinda dressing is painted in as pompous a manner, as Achilles arming':[1]

> And now, unveil'd, the *Toilet* stands display'd,
> Each Silver Vase in mystic Order laid.
> First, rob'd in White, the Nymph intent adores
> With Head uncover'd, the *Cosmetic* Pow'rs.
> A heav'nly Image in the Glass appears,
> To that she bends, to that her Eyes she rears;
> Th'inferior Priestess, at her Altar's side,
> Trembling, begins the sacred Rites of Pride.
> Unnumber'd Treasures ope at once, and here
> The various Off'rings of the World appear;
> From each she nicely culls with curious Toil,
> And decks the Goddess with the glitt'ring Spoil.
> This Casket *India*'s glowing Gems unlocks,
> And all *Arabia* breathes from yonder Box.
> The Tortoise here and Elephant unite,
> Transform'd to *Combs*, the speckled and the white.[2]

Pope delights in the 'artificial beauty' that he is describing. Yet he passes a judgement, which is expressed by the imagery of the whole passage. Just as Ben Jonson makes Volpone condemn himself out of his own mouth by apostrophizing Gold in idolatrous terms, so in the description of the toilet-table Pope shows Belinda lavishing on her own beauty the adoration which should be reserved for a higher object. Pope acknowledges the beauty of the scene, and paints it brilliantly; yet he reminds the reader that the rites he is describing are those 'of *Pride*'.[3] In the thought of the

---

[1] Warton, i. 230.   [2] i. 121–36.

[3] The word 'Pride' occurs eight times in the course of the poem, several of these being in key passages. 'Proud' and 'the Proud' also occur, as do 'Vain' and 'Vanities'.

eighteenth century pride remained the first of sins. By making it 'sacred' Belinda, and the whole *beau monde* which she represents, is guilty of a serious moral fault.

Pope's moral judgement is implicit throughout. Although the speeches of Piety and Hygeia in *Le Lutrin* and *The Dispensary* afforded precedents, it was hardly necessary for him to introduce Clarissa's speech,[1] as he did in 1717, 'to open more clearly the MORAL of the Poem'.[2]

If it had lacked a moral, explicit or implicit, *The Rape of the Lock* would have failed to meet one of the basic demands of Augustan heroic theory. Blackmore was strictly orthodox when he censured those who 'look upon an heroick Poem as only a delightful Entertainment of the Imagination by beautiful Diction and surprizing Turns, and of the Understanding by a regular and well-imagined Symmetry in the Structure', and insisted that 'Instruction and incitements to heroick Virtue, worthy Passions and generous Resolutions, are the principal Things aimed at in this Sort of Writing, without which a pretended Epick Poem, its chief End being destroyed, is an impertinent and lifeless Performance'.[3]

The demand for a 'moral' in a heroic poem was not necessarily as pedantic as it appears to most people today. A good poem, like a good play or a good novel, is never a mere chronicle of events: it has always a meaning. When the Renaissance critic inquired what the moral of an epic was, he was posing the same question as Henry James when he asked 'What is this novel *about*?' In a deep sense the moral of a poem is its significance, the expression on the countenance of the events which it describes. Its insistence on a

---

[1] v. 9–34.

[2] Pope annotated his copy of Dennis's *Remarks*. Although the details of his reply are obscure, their general direction is clear. Dennis had described *Le Lutrin* as 'a noble and important satirical Poem, upon the Luxury, the Pride, the Divisions, and Animosities of the Popish Clergy'. Pope applied this to his own poem by substituting the words 'female sex' for 'Popish Clergy'. Dennis had said that Boileau's moral was '*That when Christians, and especially the Clergy, run into great Heats about religious Trifles, their Animosity proceeds from the Want of that Religion which is the Pretence of their Quarrel*'.

For '*Clergy*', Pope wrote 'Ladies'; for '*Religion*', 'Sense'. See Tillotson, Twickenham ed., ii, pp. 368–75.

[3] Preface to *Alfred. An Epick Poem* (1723), p. vi.

moral was not the least of the ways in which the theory of
the mock-epic helped Pope to develop his occasional poem
on a lovers' tiff until it became what Warton justly called
'the BEST SATIRE extant'.[1]

[1] i. 254.

'SATIRE . . . OF THE COMICK KIND':
POPE'S *MORAL ESSAYS* AND
IMITATIONS OF HORACE

P. Libels *and* Satires! *lawless Things indeed!*
But grave Epistles, *bringing Vice to light,*
Such as a King *might read, a* Bishop *write,*
Such as Sir Robert *would approve*—F. *Indeed?*
The Case is alter'd—you may then proceed.
In such a Cause the Plaintiff will be hiss'd,
My Lords the Judges laugh, and you're dismiss'd.[1]

EXCEPT 'classical' and 'romantic' few terms in literary criticism have led to so much confusion as 'satire'. This uncertainty of definition has been largely responsible for the inadequate treatment which satirical literature has received from critics and historians. One of the objects of this book is to throw some light on the meanings of the word: the point has now come when one or two tentative distinctions may be drawn.

The Latin term *satura* refers primarily to a *form* of composition. It covers several distinct though allied species of writing 'in which prevalent follies or vices are assailed with ridicule or with serious denunciation'.[2] One type was Menippean or Varronian satire; but the principal species was the formal verse satire variously developed by Lucilius, Horace, Persius, and Juvenal. This characteristic *satura* is a poem without a plot which contains a mixture of moralizing and satire in our sense of the word. It was of this species of satire that Dryden was thinking when he pointed out that 'amongst the Romans' the word 'was not only used for those discourses which decried vice, or exposed folly, but for others also, where virtue was recommended'.[3] From first to

---

[1] *The First Satire of the Second Book*, ll. 150–6. [2] *Oxford English Dictionary.*
[3] *Essays*, ii. 67. Cf. Trapp, pp. 223–4: 'The Word *Satire* was anciently taken in a less restrain'd Sense than it is at present, not only as denoting a severe Poem against Vice, but as

last the word retained, in Latin usage, its etymological connexion with the notion of a miscellaneous composition, a
hotch-potch.

But 'in our modern languages', Dryden continues, 'we
apply [the word satire] only to invective poems, where the
very name of Satire is formidable to those persons who would
appear to the world what they are not in themselves; for in
English, to say satire, is to mean reflection, as we use that
word in the worst sense; or as the French call it, more
properly, *médisance*'.[1] The basic meaning of the word in the
seventeenth and eighteenth centuries is best understood
when one remembers that poetry and rhetoric were closely
akin. As has already been pointed out, the poet's task, like
the orator's, was to arouse in his audience certain emotions
about the subject of his poem. When scorn, hatred, or
contempt was the emotion he wished to arouse, he was
writing satire. The essence of the meaning of the word
was simply 'a composition *against* someone or something'.[2]
Whereas *satura* referred primarily to a form of composition,
satire at this period referred primarily to the poet's rhetorical
intention.[3]

Usually, of course, it was only in part of his composition
that the poet wished to arouse contempt. As a rule the scorn
which the reader was meant to feel for certain of the dramatis
personae was offset by the admiration he was intended to feel

consisting of Precepts of Virtue, and the Praises of it: And even in the Satires, as they are
call'd, of *Horace*, *Juvenal*, and *Persius*, &c. which are principally levell'd against the Weakness,
the Follies, or Vices of Mankind; we find many Directions, as well as Incitements to Virtue.
Such Strokes of Morality, *Horace*, particularly, is full of . . .'

[1] Here Dryden is following closely Dacier's *Préface sur les Satires d'Horace, Où l'on
explique l'origine & les progrés de la Satire des Romains; & tous les changemens qui luy sont
arrivez* (in vol. vi of his edition of 1681–9). 'En François', Dacier observes, 'qui dit *satire*, dit
médisance.' Préface, p. [xviii].

[2] The notion of moral purpose was not altogether forgotten in the English use of the
word. A true satire was often distinguished from a lampoon or libel by the insistence that it
should have a more than personal application and a reforming purpose. Conversely, Johnson
defined 'lampoon' as 'A personal satire; abuse; censure written not to reform but to vex'.

[3] One reason for confusion about the meaning of the word *satire* was the false derivation
from Gk. σάτυρος. Although Casaubon exploded this in his great work *De Satyrica Graecorum
Poesi, & Romanorum Satira Libri duo* (1605), which Dryden knew, the association of satire
with invective and abuse, for which the old derivation was partly responsible, continued. As
Dacier and Dryden noted, the false derivation was reflected in the spelling *satyr*.

for others. But when (as in *Absalom and Achitophel*) the principal object of the poet was to attack, the whole composition was termed a satire. For this reason it is misleading to speak of 'the style of satire'. The style varied from passage to passage with the rhetorical intention.

The fundamental difference of meaning between *satura* and *satire* is thrown into relief by the fact that the Latin word, unlike the English, was never used to refer to passages of incidental satire in a composition of some other species. The Latin equivalent for this use of the English 'satire' would be some such word as *irrisio*, *vituperatio*, or *acerbitas*: never *satura*.[1] It is because the word in English has never referred primarily to a definite form of writing that it now used indifferently for any literary work which portrays a particular person, or human life itself, in a highly unsympathetic manner. 'Satire' now relates to the mode of a writer's vision, the temper of his writing. The main vehicle for satire recently has been the novel.

II

The remarkable scarcity of formal verse satire in the Augustan age makes nonsense of the charge that it was a period of unintelligent imitation of the classics. None of the satires examined so far has been modelled on the Latin *satura*. It is now time to turn to the poems which are, with *The Vanity of Human Wishes*, the most successful formal verse satires of the period.[2]

Shaftesbury had the distinction between *satura* and *satire* in his mind when he wrote in his *Soliloquy: or Advice to an Author*: 'Our *Satyr* ... is scurrilous, buffooning, and without Morals or Instruction; which is the Majesty and Life of this kind of writing.'[3] Pope would have assented in this

[1] J. Wight Duff, *Roman Satire: Its Outlook on Social Life* (1937) is my authority for this and for several other statements in this section. See particularly pp. 12–13.

[2] The texts quoted in this chapter are those of the Twickenham edition, vol. III, ii (1951), ed. F. W. Bateson, and vol. IV (1939), ed. John Butt.

[3] *Characteristicks, &c.*, 1711, i. 266. It seems certain that the *Advice to an Author*, which appeared when he was twenty-two, exerted a considerable influence on Pope.

judgement. 'I have not the courage . . . to be such a satirist as you', he wrote to Swift, 'but I would be as much, or more, a philosopher. You call your satires, libels: I would rather call my satires, epistles. They will consist more of morality than of wit, and grow graver, which you will call duller. I shall leave it to my antagonists to be witty, if they can, and content myself to be useful, and in the right.'[1] Pope's aim in the *Moral Essays* and the *Imitations of Horace* was that attributed to Horace in Dacier's edition:

> Dans ces deux Livres [Dacier had written], Horace veut nous apprendre à combatre nos vices, à regler nos passions, à suivre la Nature, pour donner des bornes à nos desirs; à démêler le faux d'avec le vray, & nos idées d'avec les choses: à revenir de nos préjugez; à bien connoistre les principes & les motifs de toutes nos actions, & à éviter le ridicule qui se trouve dans tous les hommes entêtez des opinions qu'ils ont receuës de leur Maîtres, & qu'ils retiennent opiniâtrément, sans examiner si elles sont bien fondées. En un mot, il travaille à nous rendre heureux pour nous-mesmes, agreables & fideles à nos amis, & commodes, discrets, & honnêtes, pour tous ceux avec qui nous sommes obligez de vivre.[2]

The Latin *satura* is in essence an informal ethical epistle, without a plot,[3] in which the poet teaches by precept and by examples.[4] The form is such a free one[5] that there is no difficulty in considering the *Moral Essays* and the *Imitations of Horace* equally as examples. The principal difference

---

[1] *E.-C.* vii. 306. This applies equally to the *Moral Essays* and the *Imitations of Horace.* Pope's comments on his own work in letters often exaggerate one aspect of the truth according to the whim of the moment. Here he minimizes the element of attack in these poems.

[2] pp. [xxii–xxiii] of the *Préface.*

[3] It may be of interest to give Heinsius's definition of Horatian satire in full: 'Satyra est poësis, sine actionum serie, ad purgandos hominum animos inuenta. in qua vitia humana, ignorantia, ac errores, tum quae ex utrisque proveniunt, in singulis, partim dramatico, partim simplici, partim mixto ex utroque genere dicendi, occulte utplurimum ac figurate, perstringuntur: sicut humili ac familiari, ita acri partim ac dicaci, partim urbano ac iocoso constans sermone. quibus odium, indignatio mouetur, aut risus.' *De Satyra Horatiana Libri duo* (1629), p. 54.

[4] Horace did not entitle any of his works *Saturae.* He used the terms *Sermones* and *Epistolae.* There is an interesting essay 'On Epistolary Writing' in vol. i of Hurd's ed. of Horace's *Epistolae ad Pisones, et Augustum* (4th ed., 1766).

[5] See Mary Claire Randolph: 'The Structural Design of the Formal Verse Satire' (*P.Q.* Oct. 1942), a useful article which cites numerous discussions in classical journals.

between the two groups of poems lies in their arrangement. The *Moral Essays* observe what Dryden called 'this important secret, in the designing of a perfect satire; that it ought only to treat of one subject; to be confined to one particular theme; or at least, to one principally'.[1] In the *Imitations of Horace*, on the other hand, Pope abandoned the unity of theme observed by Persius, Boileau, and Edward Young in favour of the more informal *causerie* of Horace.

If the success of Young's seven 'Characteristical Satires', collected in 1728 as *Love of Fame, the Universal Passion*, was one reason for the comparatively systematic arrangement of Pope's *Moral Essays*,[2] another was the influence of Warburton. 'When the Editor, at the Author's desire, first examined this Epistle', he wrote in the notes to the first *Moral Essay* for the *Works* of 1751, 'he was surprized to find it contain a number of fine observations, without order, connexion, or dependence: but much more so, when, on an attentive review, he saw, that, if put into a different form, on an idea he then conceived, it would have all the clearness of method, and force of connected reasoning.' Accordingly 'the order and disposition of the several parts' of the poem were 'entirely changed and transposed, tho' with hardly the Alteration of a single Word'. So it came about that the four poems which we now know as the *Moral Essays* are more closely related to the ill-fated scheme for 'a *short* yet not *imperfect* system of Ethics'[3] than are the later *Imitations of Horace*.

[1] *Essays*, ii. 102.

[2] See Charlotte E. Crawford: 'What was Pope's Debt to Edward Young?' (*E.L.H.* Sept. 1946). Miss Crawford sees the influence of Young in all of the *Moral Essays* except the one first published (that to Burlington, now known as 'IV').

[3] 'The Design' prefixed to the *Essay on Man*.

In accordance with Pope's usual practice, lines, couplets, and longer passages were interchanged between the *Essay on Man*, the *Moral Essays*, the *Imitations of Horace*, and *The Dunciad* during their composition. In particular the poems examined in this chapter were enriched with many strokes of satire which decorum obliged Pope to excise from the more dignified *Essay on Man*. See George Sherburn, 'Pope at Work', in *Essays on the Eighteenth Century Presented to David Nichol Smith* (1945), p. 60.

III

By choosing Horace as his model Pope was adding his voice to a discussion which was already old in his time. The debate about the respective merits of Horace and Juvenal was a specialized form of the argument about the whole nature and status of satire. In this argument the poets and critics of the seventeenth and eighteenth centuries were the successors of the scholars of the Renaissance, who had already established practically every point with which the modern reader is familiar in the pages of Dryden, Pope, and Johnson. The success of Dryden's *Discourse concerning the Original and Progress of Satire* was largely due to the fact that it summarized, conveniently and in brilliant prose, a debate which had already been carried on, in Latin and the various vernacular languages, for more than a century.

One of the most intelligent treatments of the main point at issue, that of the style and tone most suitable in satire, may be found in Dennis's letter *To Matthew Prior, Esq; Upon the Roman Satirists* (1721):

There can be no true Preference [Dennis wrote] where there can be no just Comparison, and ... there can be no just Comparison between Authors whose Works are not *ejusdem generis*, and ... the Works of those two Satirists are not *ejusdem generis*. For do not you believe, Sir, that Mr. *Dryden* is in the wrong where he affirms that the *Roman* Satire had its Accomplishment in *Juvenal*? For is there not Reason to believe that the true *Roman* Satire is of the Comick Kind, and was an Imitation of the old *Athenian* Comedys, in which *Lucilius* first signaliz'd himself, and which was afterwards perfected by *Horace*, and that *Juvenal* afterwards started a new Satire which was of the Tragick kind? *Horace*, who wrote as *Lucilius* had done before him, in Imitation of the old Comedy, endeavours to correct the Follies and Errors, and epidemick Vices of his Readers, which is the Business of Comedy. *Juvenal* attacks the pernicious outragious Passions and the abominable monstrous Crimes of several of his Contemporaries ... which is the Business of Tragedy, at least of imperfect Tragedy. *Horace* argues, insinuates, engages, rallies, smiles; *Juvenal* exclaims, apostrophizes, exaggerates, lashes, stabbs. There is in *Horace* almost every where an

agreeable Mixture·of good Sense, and of true Pleasantry, so that he
has every where the principal Qualities of an excellent Comick Poet.
And there is almost every where in *Juvenal*, Anger, Indignation, Rage,
Disdain, and the violent Emotions and vehement Style of Tragedy.[1]

A further account of the Horatian species of satire may
be found in the *Spectator*. 'The Qualifications requisite for
writing Epistles, after the Model given us by *Horace*', are
described in No. 618.

He that would excel in this kind must have a good Fund of strong
Masculine Sense: To this there must be joined a thorough Knowledge
of Mankind, together with an Insight into the Business, and the
prevailing Humours of the Age. Our Author must have his Mind well
seasoned with the finest Precepts of Morality, and be filled with nice
Reflections upon the bright and the dark sides of human Life: He
must be a Master of refined Raillery, and understand the Delicacies,
as well as the Absurdities of Conversation. He must have a lively Turn
of Wit, with an easie and concise manner of Expression; Every thing
he says, must be in a free and disengaged manner. He must be guilty of
nothing that betrays the Air of a Recluse, but appear a Man of the
World throughout.

It is clear that when Bolingbroke suggested that Pope
should imitate the First Satire of the Second Book of Horace
he was pointing him to the right model. Juvenal and his
modern imitators did not greatly appeal to Pope (in a reveal-
ing aside he once told Spence that Oldham was 'a very
indelicate writer'[2]). He prided himself on differing from
Dryden in being 'genteel', in mixing with courtiers and wits
rather than only with 'poetical men';[3] it was in the manner of
Horace rather than Juvenal that men of such good breeding
could most properly be addressed.[4]

By making Horace his model, and thereby choosing
ridicule as one of the main weapons for his campaign against
bad taste and immorality, Pope was once again (whether
consciously or not) following the course recommended by
Shaftesbury, who had pointed out that didactic writing

[1] Hooker, ii. 218–19.   [2] p. 19.
[3] Spence, p. 261.
[4] See the further passage from Dennis quoted below, on p. 137.

has so little Force towards the winning our Attention, that it is apter
to tire us, than the Metre of an old Ballad. . . . The only Manner left,
in which Criticism can have its just Force amongst us, is the *antient*
COMICK; of which kind were the first *Roman* Miscellanys, or *Satyrick*
Pieces: a sort of original Writing of their own, refin'd afterwards by
the best Genius, and politest Poet of that Nation; who, notwithstand-
ing, owns the Manner to have been taken from the *Greek* Comedy
above-mention'd. . . . If our home-Wits wou'd refine upon this
Pattern, they might perhaps meet with considerable Success.[1]

One caution is necessary. In making Horace his model
and electing to write 'comick' satire Pope was in no sense
repudiating moral seriousness; nor did he limit himself to
minor offenders. As a passage in the *Epilogue to the Satires*
makes clear, he distrusted those who claimed that Horace

> . . . was delicate, was nice;
> *Bubo* observes, he lash'd no sort of *Vice*.[2]

Pope despised this argument as the refuge of men who feared
the lash of satire; his own Horatian satires contain passages
of direct attack and bitter denunciation.

IV

Although the modern reader is apt to think of the
Imitations of Horace and the *Moral Essays* as belonging to the
same class of poetry as Dryden's 'satires', they are written
in an entirely different style. Instead of the heroic style of
Absalom and Achitophel we find in them an informal and
familiar idiom which may be regarded as a highly personal
development of the middle style of writing, with occasional
affinities both to the more elevated style and (more often)
the low style.[3]

Since this kind of writing was allied to comedy, the
movement of the verse lacks the dignified march characteristic of Dryden's heroic idiom; instead of the 'numbers' of

---

[1] *Characteristicks*, i. 258–9.   [2] *Dialogue I*, ll. 11–12.
[3] Trapp says that in Horatian Satire 'a common [i.e. "Middle"] Style is the general Rule,
tho' there may be some Exceptions to it', p. 230 n. Cf. 'Praise cannot stoop, *like Satire, to the
Ground*'. *Epilogue, Dialogue II*, l. 110 (my italics). Dryden had written: 'The low style of
Horace is according to his subject, that is, generally grovelling.' *Essays*, ii. 85.

high style we find swift-moving verse that forms a perfect
vehicle for a witty *causerie*.

Because the style is seldom elevated the versification is
important; for it is largely on the management of rhythm
and the functional use of rhyme that this idiom depends for
such dignity as it possesses. Here Jonson, Donne, and other
early writers who might have been eligible models broke
down; it was necessary, rather, to follow the example of
Waller and Rochester. 'Most of the pieces which are usually
produced upon this plan', the author of *The Letters of Sir
Thomas Fitzosborne* was later to complain, 'rather give one
an image of Lucilius, than of Horace: the authors of them
seem to mistake the aukward negligence of the favorite of
Scipio, for the easy air of the friend of Maecenas.'[1] Perhaps
Horace himself was sometimes 'too negligent of his Versification';[2] that was no argument for carelessness on the
part of the modern poet. Right conduct in this matter may
be studied in the practice of Pope. There are few run-on
lines; the sense is usually complete within the single pentameter; while the rhyme serves to give pattern to the prosaic
diction and predominantly colloquial ordering of the words.

A similar mean is to be observed in the choice of words.
That 'natural ease of expression' expected of this style
'consists in . . . an elegant familiarity of phrase, which tho
formed of the most usual terms of language, has yet a grace
and energy, no less striking than that of a more elevated
diction'.[3] This requirement is exactly met by the opening of
The First Epistle of the First Book:

> ST JOHN, whose love indulg'd my labours past,
> Matures my present, and shall bound my last!
> Why will you break the Sabbath of my days?
> Now sick alike of Envy and of Praise.

Pope had read in Dryden's *Discourse* that Casaubon objected
to Horace's satires on the score of excessive meanness: 'He
says that Horace, being the son of a tax-gatherer, or a

---

[1] *Fitzosborne Letters*, No. xxxvii.   [2] The *Spectator*, No. 618.
[3] *Fitzosborne Letters*, No. xxxvii.

collector, as we call it, smells everywhere of the meanness of his birth and education: his conceits are vulgar, like the subjects of his satires; that he does *plebeium sapere*, and writes not with that elevation which becomes a satirist.'[1] As has been said, however, Pope followed the critics[2] who believed that this familiarity of word and phrase was intentional, and rightly belonged to the kind of writing that Horace was practising. In his Horatian poems Pope deliberately used mean words much more frequently than words of a poetical cast: instead of such phrases as 'incumbent Sky', 'pale-ey'd virgins', 'a sad variety of woe' and 'moss-grown domes' one finds 'Meat, Cloaths, and Fire', 'Sappho at her toilet's greazy task', drops and nostrums and boiled eggs.[3]

The prevalent diction is rather familiar than low. In particular one notices the predominance of 'Saxon' words. When Pope censured the 'ten low words' that 'creep in one dull line' in the *Essay on Criticism*,[4] he was thinking primarily of poetry which aimed at elevation. In this familiar sort of verse short words are proper, as they form the staple of everyday conversation:

> I was not born for Courts or great Affairs,
> I pay my Debts, believe, and say my Pray'rs,
> Can sleep without a Poem in my head,
> Nor know, if *Dennis* be alive or dead.[5]

A fine example of diction perfectly suited to the sense occurs in *The First Epistle of the Second Book*, where Pope follows Horace in praising the past:

> Time was, a sober Englishman wou'd knock
> His servants up, and rise by five a clock,
> Instruct his Family in ev'ry rule,
> And send his Wife to Church, his Son to school.[6]

---

[1] *Essays*, ii. 77.

[2] Such as Vossius, who rules that 'The Diction of Satire . . . ought to resemble Prose rather than Poetry, and appear with as much Ease as if it flow'd *Extempore*. . . .' (Quoted in Trapp, p. 229.)

[3] *The Temple of Fame*, 58; *Eloisa to Abelard*, 21, 36, 142; *Moral Essays*, iii. 82; ibid. ii. 25; *Epistle to Arbuthnot*, 29; and *Epistles*, ii. ii. 85.   [4] l. 347.

[5] *Epistle to Arbuthnot*, ll. 267–70.   [6] ll. 161–4.

This familiar diction enables Pope to introduce mean detail without incongruity and often with brilliant effect, as when he proclaims that he never

> . . . like a Puppy daggled thro' the Town,
> To fetch and carry Sing-song up and down;
> Nor at Rehearsals sweat, and mouth'd, and cry'd,
> With Handkerchief and Orange at my side.[1]

It is unusual in most sorts of poetry for the arrangement of the words to approximate to that of prose for more than a few words at a time. Here the *Imitations* and the *Moral Essays* are quite exceptional:

> What will a Child learn sooner than a song?
> What better teach a Foreigner the tongue?
> What's long or short, each accent where to place,
> And speak in publick with some sort of grace.
> I scarce can think him such a worthless thing,
> Unless he praise some monster of a King.[2]

Here, except in the third line, the words are almost exactly in the order of conversation. This is true of many of the more matter-of-fact passages in these poems.

The poet's 'Illustrations [and] Comparisons', wrote the author of the *Spectator* essay, '. . . must be drawn from common Life'. As might be expected images from 'low' aspects of life are particularly frequent in the satirical passages. The Fox brothers are 'like . . . as one Egg to another'; a miser's soul 'still sits at squat, and peeps not from its hole'; the monument with an inscription blaming the Papists for the Fire of London 'like a tall bully, lifts the head, and lyes'; while the stench of a barbecued hog is 'rank as the ripeness of a Rabbit's tail'.[3] Such brief conceits, limited to a single

---

[1] *Epistle to Arbuthnot*, ll. 225 et seq. Another good example of this sort of realism occurs at the end of *The First Epistle of the Second Book*:

> . . . When I flatter, let my dirty leaves
> (Like Journals, Odes, and such forgotten things
> As Eusden, Philips, Settle, writ of Kings)
> Cloath spice, line trunks, or flutt'ring in a row,
> Befringe the rails of Bedlam and Sohoe.

The effect is close to that of Swift's familiar verse.

[2] *Epistles*, ii. i, ll. 205–10.

[3] *Satires*, ii. i. 50; *Moral Essays*, i. 115; ibid. iii. 340; *Satires*, ii. ii. 28.

line or couplet, are the most characteristic images in these
poems, and the most successful. More elaborate figures are
rare:

> Long, as to him who works for debt, the Day;
> Long as the Night to her whose love's away;
> Long as the Year's dull circle seems to run,
> When the brisk Minor pants for twenty-one;
> So slow th'unprofitable Moments roll,
> That lock up all the Functions of my soul.[1]

Although effective in itself, this string of similes is a shade
too heroic for the Horatian manner.

When imagery grows plentiful it is usually a sign of strong
feeling. The 'character' of Sporus, which is a tissue of 'mean'
images,[2] is a notable example:

> Yet let me flap this Bug with gilded wings,
> This painted Child of Dirt that stinks and stings;
> Whose Buzz the Witty and the Fair annoys,
> Yet Wit ne'er tastes, and Beauty ne'er enjoys,
> So wel-bred Spaniels civilly delight
> In mumbling of the Game they dare not bite.
> Eternal Smiles his Emptiness betray,
> As shallow streams run dimpling all the way.
> Whether in florid Impotence he speaks,
> And, as the Prompter breathes, the Puppet squeaks;
> Or at the Ear of *Eve*, familiar Toad,
> Half Froth, half Venom, spits himself abroad,
> In Puns, or Politicks, or Tales, or Lyes,
> Or Spite, or Smut, or Rymes, or Blasphemies.
> His Wit all see-saw between *that* and *this*,
> Now high, now low, now Master up, now Miss,
> And he himself one vile Antithesis.[3]

In such a passage the unanswerable quality of a perfect
image is manifest. Whether the statements are true or false
in fact, the success of the imagery proclaims their imaginative

---

[1] *Epistles*, i. i. 35–40.

[2] When Johnson says that 'The meanest passage is the satire upon Sporus' (*Lives*, iii.
246), he is using the word in its semi-technical sense.

[3] *Epistle to Arbuthnot*, ll. 309–25. Note the use of the final triplet to lead up to a rhetorical
climax.

truth against all denial. Hatred has never dictated more lethal
images.

V

The variety of these poems in subject, emotion, and tone
deserves to be emphasized. Literary criticism alternates with
general satire, panegyric with personal censure,[1] autobiography with moralizing. And such is Pope's mastery of
style that the idiom is everywhere subtly adapted to the
nature of the passage. Beside passages reminiscent of the
Essay on Man—

> Ask we what makes one keep, and one bestow?
> That POW'R who bids the Ocean ebb and flow,
> Bids seed-time, harvest, equal course maintain,
> Thro' reconcil'd extremes of drought and rain,
> Builds Life on Death, on Change Duration founds,
> And gives th' eternal wheels to know their rounds[2]

—there is the brilliant satiric realism of the portrait of Villiers, in which the clogged and hindered utterance reminds
one of Donne:

> In the worst inn's worst room, with mat half-hung,
> The floors of plaister, and the walls of dung,
> On once a flock-bed, but repair'd with straw,
> With tape-ty'd curtains, never meant to draw,
> The George and Garter dangling from that bed
> Where tawdry yellow strove with dirty red,
> Great Villiers lies—alas! how chang'd from him
> That life of pleasure, and that soul of whim!
> Gallant and gay, in Cliveden's proud alcove,
> The bow'r of wanton Shrewsbury and love.[3]

Beside the cruel antitheses of the lines on Addison and the
controlled savagery of the Sporus passage one finds the
perfectly turned compliments to friends and the moving lines
on the poet's parents and the 'blameless' Gay.

---

[1] The role of panegyrist was traditionally 'doubled' with that of satirist. '*Boileau*, like
Horace, was born equally for *Satyr* and for *Praise*', Ozell wrote in the dedication of his
translation of *Le Lutrin* (1708).

[2] *Moral Essays*, iii. 165–70.   [3] Ibid. 299–308.

Although the characteristic level of style in 'this middle
way of writing' is unpretentious, it was generally recognized
that 'Subjects of the most sublime Nature are often treated
in the Epistolary way with Advantage'.[1] On such occasions
'the Poet surprizes us with his Pomp, and seems rather be-
trayed into his Subject, than to have aimed at it by design:
He appears like the Visit of a King *Incognito*, with a mixture
of Familiarity, and Grandeur'. Such elevated passages occur
most frequently when Pope is moralizing:

> Man? and *for ever*? Wretch! what wou'dst thou have?
> Heir urges Heir, like Wave impelling Wave:
> All vast Possessions (just the same the case
> Whether you call them Villa, Park, or Chace)
> Alas! my BATHURST! what will they avail?
> Join *Cotswold* Hills to *Saperton's* fair Dale,
> Let rising Granaries and Temples here,
> There mingled Farms and Pyramids appear,
> Link Towns to Towns with Avenues of Oak,
> Enclose whole Downs in Walls, 'tis all a joke!
> Inexorable Death shall level all,
> And Trees, and Stones, and Farms, and Farmer fall.[2]

Johnson might have envied the eloquent pessimism of these
lines.

It is often when he is most personal and autobiographical
that Pope's tone in these poems becomes most elevated:

> What? arm'd for *Virtue* when I point the Pen,
> Brand the bold Front of shameless, guilty Men,
> Dash the proud Gamester in his gilded Car,
> Bare the mean Heart that lurks beneath a Star;
> Can there be wanting to defend Her Cause,
> Lights of the Church, or Guardians of the Laws?
> Could pension'd *Boileau* lash in honest Strain
> Flatt'rers and Bigots ev'n in *Louis*' Reign?
> Could Laureate *Dryden* Pimp and Fry'r engage,
> Yet neither *Charles* nor *James* be in a Rage?
> And I not strip the Gilding off a Knave,
> Un-plac'd, un-pension'd, no Man's Heir, or Slave?[3]

---

[1] *Spectator*, No. 618.   [2] *Epistles*, II. ii. 252–63.   [3] *Satires*, II. i. 105–16.

In such a passage, where 'the sentiments . . . [are] enforced with all the strength of eloquence and poetry',[1] it is an education in the methods of a great poet to watch the subtle changes which appear in the arrangement of the words, and the almost spontaneous occurrence of personifications and rhetorical questions as an accompaniment to the tautened verse and more condensed thought. When such features of poetic rhetoric appear—along with elaborate similes, descriptions and sharp antitheses—it is a sure sign that the poet's emotion is very strong.[2]

Whereas Dryden, the least personal of poets, followed the example of Juvenal, Pope found his true exemplar in Horace, who is much more given to poetic autobiography. It was the fact that Horace afforded a precedent for dramatized self-expression that made him a perfect model for Pope. The theme of the poet's *apologia* runs through the *Imitations of Horace*[3] as constantly as the vein of literary satire. Pope increased its rhetorical effectiveness by making a skilled use of the conventionalized dialogue which has been associated with the *satura* from the earliest times:

F.   . . . Spare then the Person, and expose the Vice.
P.   How Sir! not damn the Sharper, but the Dice?
       Come on then Satire! gen'ral, unconfin'd,
       Spread thy broad wing, and sowze on all the Kind.
       Ye Statesmen, Priests, of one Religion all!
       Ye Tradesmen vile, in Army, Court, or Hall!
       Ye Rev'rend Atheists!— F. Scandal! name them, Who?
P.   Why that's the thing you bid me not to do.
       Who starv'd a Sister, who forswore a Debt,

---

[1] *Fitzosborne Letters*, No. xxxvii.

[2] Notice, for example, the personifications near the end of the Second Dialogue of the *Epilogue to the Satires*:

> Let Envy howl while Heav'n's whole Chorus sings,
> And bark at Honour not confer'd by Kings;
> Let Flatt'ry sickening see the Incense rise,
> Sweet to the World, and grateful to the Skies:
> Truth guards the Poet, sanctifies the line,
> And makes Immortal, Verse as mean as mine.   (242–7)

Particularly severe passages of satire are often distinguished by sharp antitheses.

[3] One of the main differences between the *Moral Essays* and the *Imitations of Horace* is that the personal element is more prominent in the latter.

> I never nam'd—the Town's enquiring yet.
> The pois'ning Dame— *Fr*. You mean— *P*. I don't—
>   *Fr*. You do.
> *P*.   See! now I keep the Secret, and not you.
>   The bribing Statesman— *Fr*. Hold! too high you go.
> *P*.   The brib'd Elector— *Fr*. There you stoop too low.[1]

The use of dialogue here is intensely dramatic. The couplets are split with brilliant effect: the result is to emphasize, by opposition, the intensely personal note.

Those of the *Moral Essays* and the *Imitations of Horace* which are not dialogues are epistles addressed to friends; and it is of the essence of an epistle to be a dramatic monologue. The poet's correspondent, with his own tastes and prejudices, is a felt presence in the background.[2] This helps Pope to attain a tension in his verse which proclaims its kinship with drama.

Perfect control of tone was a matter to which Pope devoted a great deal of care; he realized that it was one of the last mysteries of the art of poetry. Almost always in these poems his tone is perfectly adjusted to the requirements of the moment. This very perfection makes his one or two apparent lapses particularly interesting. One such fault has already been pointed out: the string of similes in *The First Epistle of the First Book*. Another occurs in the second paragraph of the *Epistle to Dr. Arbuthnot*:

> What Walls can guard me, or what Shades can hide?
> They pierce my Thickets, thro' my Grot they glide,
> By land, by water, they renew the charge,
> They stop the Chariot, and they board the Barge.

---

[1] *Epilogue to the Satires, Dialogue II*, ll. 12–25. There is an interesting study of Pope's forensic skill, principally in the *Epistle to Arbuthnot*, by Elder Olson: 'Rhetoric and the Appreciation of Pope', *M.P.* Aug. 1939. But Mr. Olson is wrong in supposing that rhetoric and poetry are mutually exclusive.

[2] The fact that the distinction between epistle and dialogue was purely one of rhetorical structure and convenience is emphasized by the fact that Pope changed the third *Moral Essay* from an epistle to a dialogue: 'The late Lord BATHURST, told me', Warton wrote, '"that he was much surprized to see what he had with repeated pleasure so often read as an *epistle* addressed to himself, in this edition converted into a *dialogue*; in which", said he, "I perceive I really make but a shabby and indifferent figure".' *Essay*, ii. 158. The change may have been made at the suggestion of Warburton: see the Twickenham editor's Introduction, p. xvi, and pp. 76–77 of his edition.

One's first reaction to these lines is to judge that they are too heroic for this sort of verse: their exclamatory note is very rare in Pope's Horatian poems.[1] And even when one realizes that the intention is mock-heroic the judgement that the passage is not perfectly in key still stands.

It is instructive to notice the way in which Pope 'imitated' *The First Epistle of the Second Book*, which was generally regarded as the most elevated of Horace's *Epistles*.[2] Instead of simply adopting the tone of the original, he turned it to irony; so that the opening of the poem, and a number of other passages, are examples of what might be termed the mock-heroic-epistolary style:

> While You, great Patron of Mankind, sustain
> The balanc'd World, and open all the Main;
> Your Country, chief, in Arms abroad defend,
> At home, with Morals, Arts, and Laws amend;
> How shall the Muse, from such a Monarch, steal
> An hour, and not defraud the Publick Weal?

---

[1] It may be due partly to the example of Young. See, for example, his first *Epistle to Mr. Pope, Concerning the Authors of the Age* (1730).

Melmoth's judgement that the exclamatory should be avoided in this species of writing is clear when (in the passage already referred to on p. 7, n. 4) he contrasts the following lines from Pope's version of *The First Satire of the Second Book*—

> Peace is my dear Delight—not *Fleury's* more:
> But touch me, and no Minister so sore.
> Whoe'er offends, at some unlucky Time
> Slides into Verse, and hitches in a Rhyme,
> Sacred to Ridicule! his whole Life long,
> And the sad Burthen of some merry Song   (ll. 75–80)

—with a translation of the same passage by another (unnamed) poet:

> Behold me blameless bard, how fond of peace!
> But he who hurts me (nay, I will be heard)
> Had better take a lion by the beard;
> His eyes shall weep the folly of his tongue,
> By laughing crouds in rueful ballad sung.

'There is a strength and spirit in the former of these passages', Melmoth comments, 'and a flatness and languor in the latter, which cannot fail of being discovered.' What is wrong is that the latter passage, though it has some good things in it, 'is much too solemn and tragical for the undisturbed pleasantry of Horace' and of the Horatian epistle in general. See the remarks of Pope quoted on p. 7.

[2] Dryden remarks that this Epistle 'is of so much dignity in the words, and of so much elegancy in the numbers, that the author plainly shows the *sermo pedestris*, in his other Satires, was rather his choice than his necessity'. *Essays*, ii. 85.

Like the opening of *MacFlecknoe* these lines might be perfectly straightforward heroic verse; but when the circumstances are known all is turned to irony.[1] A passage in the
Epistle to Arbuthnot comes to mind:

> One dedicates, in high Heroic prose,
> And ridicules beyond a hundred foes.[2]

To address George II in the manner which Horace considered appropriate to Augustus was indeed to 'ridicule beyond
a hundred foes'.[3]

---

[1] The irony is practically confined to the opening of this poem and a passage near the end;
otherwise there are only one or two ironical touches.

[2] ll. 109–10.

[3] In the fourth satire of *The Universal Passion* Young had seriously applied Horace's praise
of Augustus to George I.

VII

THE DUNCIAD

The Vertues required in an Heroick Poem, and indeed in all Writings published, are comprehended all in this one word, Discretion.
And Discretion consisteth in this, That every part of the Poem be conducing, and in good order placed, to the End and Designe of the Poet.

THOMAS HOBBES[1]

J. M. ROBERTSON pointed out that many critics had gone astray in their interpretation of *Hamlet* 'by ignoring what ought to be very obvious; that *Hamlet* is a stratification, that it represents the efforts of a series of men, each making what he could out of the work of his predecessors'.[2] Something similar is true of *The Dunciad*, except that in this instance Pope himself at different points in his career takes the place of the 'series of men'. There is little likelihood of understanding *The Dunciad* unless it is approached with some knowledge of the various forms in which its component parts were first written and published.

Unfortunately the first stage in the composition of the poem is unknown. It seems unlikely that Theobald was the original hero; but who his predecessor was we do not know. Perhaps the original motive of the poem—or one of its original motives—was to satirize the incompetence in matters of 'wit' and taste of the official, bourgeois mind —whether that of the City of London (in choosing their City Poet) or that of the Government (in the choice of a Laureate).[3]

[1] Preface to his translation of the *Odyssey* (1675), in Spingarn, ii. 67. All quotations from *The Dunciad* in this chapter are from the (A) and (B) texts as given in vol. v of the Twickenham edition, edited by James Sutherland.

[2] T. S. Eliot's summary of Robertson's theory, in *Selected Essays* (ed. of 1934), p. 142.

[3] See George Sherburn, *The Best of Pope* (1940), p. 450, for the suggestion that *The Dunciad* began as a satire on the election of a City Poet.

In a general sense, *MacFlecknoe* was a precedent for a satire on the taste of the ill-informed in poetry. If, as is likely, Pope shared the common misconception that *MacFlecknoe*

Since there is no certain information about the 'Ur-Dunciad'—that shadow of a shade—it is with the Dunciad of 1728, in three Books, that the critic must begin. There is no doubt that the model of the poem as it was then published was MacFlecknoe. Like Dryden's poem, the Dunciad of 1728 describes the succession of one dunce to another on the throne of Dulness. The general resemblance is particularly evident in Book I, at the opening of Book II, and in the design of Book III.

Yet it is clear that Pope's object is not identical with Dryden's—attack on a personal enemy by means of ridicule. For after the description of Theobald simpering self-consciously on an immense throne in the opening lines he is a mere spectator for the rest of Book II, which is devoted to the 'high, heroic Games' in which booksellers and other bad writers celebrate his coronation. It is clear that Pope wished to satirize not only Theobald but a host of bad writers, ignorant patrons, and unscrupulous publishers.

For the social historian The Dunciad is of exceptional interest. 'We shall next declare the occasion and the cause which moved our Poet to this particular work', Martinus Scriblerus remarks in his preface.

He lived in those days, when (after providence had permitted the Invention of Printing as a scourge for the Sins of the learned) Paper also became so cheap, and printers so numerous, that a deluge of authors cover'd the land: Whereby not only the peace of the honest unwriting subject was daily molested, but unmerciful demands were made of his applause, yea of his money, by such as would neither earn the one, or deserve the other: At the same time, the Liberty of the Press was so unlimited, that it grew dangerous to refuse them

celebrated Shadwell's inauguration as Poet Laureate (see, for example, Johnson's Lives, i. 383), Dryden's poem must have appeared an even closer model.

If we knew the original motive of The Dunciad we should be in a better position to guess which part of the poem as we have it was written first. Courthope (E.-C. iv. 8) and R. K. Root (The Poetical Career of Alexander Pope (1938), p. 153) conjecture that Book III was the first to be written. Another possibility is (A) I. 83 et seq.:

'Twas on the day, when Thorold, rich and grave,
Like Cimon triumph'd, both on land and wave:
(Pomps without guilt, of bloodless swords and maces,
Glad chains, warm furs, broad banners, and broad faces) . . .

either. . . . Our author . . . did conceive it an endeavour well worthy
an honest satyrist, to dissuade the dull and punish the malicious, *the
only way that was left*. In that public-spirited view he laid the plan of
this Poem.

Considering that Dulness and Poverty are the causes of bad
authors, he cast about for a subject to illustrate their power;

and none cou'd be more so than that which our poet hath chosen, the
introduction of the lowest diversions of the rabble in *Smithfield* to be
the entertainment of the court and town; or in other words, the Action
of the Dunciad is the Removal of the Imperial seat of Dulness from the
City to the polite world.[1]

When a poet professes to have had more objects than one
in the composition of a poem, it is always difficult to assess
their relative importance; but there is no reason to doubt that
the increasing prominence of journalism and the production
of books simply as a marketable commodity was one of
Pope's targets. *The Dunciad* is not only an attack on bad
writers and bad writing: it is Pope's pessimistic commentary
on an important development of the civilization of his time.
It is a bitter protest against the levelling-down of literary
standards. This aspect of the poem may have grown directly
out of its early object of satirizing Official Poets.

Unlike the authors of *Le Lutrin* and *The Dispensary*, Pope
was not presented with a plot by actual occurrences: he had
to invent one. Dryden had had to do this for *MacFlecknoe*;
but aiming only to write a short poem he had little difficulty.
Pope's problem was closer to Butler's. Whether *Hudibras*
could ever have been made into a satisfactory whole is very
doubtful: *The Dunciad*, certainly, was not. The principal
incidents on which it is built—the coronation of Theobald,
the heroic games, and the vision—are not connected in any
satisfactory manner.

From the first Pope seems to have been doubtful whether
Theobald was a suitable hero for his poem. His role, no
doubt, is similar to that of Bayes in *The Rehearsal*: he is

---

[1] pp. 49–51 in the Twickenham edition (Pope's italics).

intended to serve as an image of that which is being attacked throughout the poem, much as an effigy of the Pope used to represent all that was most repugnant to Englishmen in Roman Catholicism.[1]

The nature of *The Dunciad* of 1728, therefore, is accurately suggested by the lines from Spenser which Pope at one time intended to prefix to it:

> A cloud of cumbrous gnats do him molest,
> All striving to enfix their feeble stings;
> That from their noyance, he no where can rest:
> But with his clownish hands their tender wings
> He brusheth oft; and oft doth mar their murmurings.[2]

Perhaps it is because it is seldom read until after the later version that the exclusively literary bearing of the 1728 *Dunciad* is so often overlooked. To say that in the four-book version the amount of moral and political satire is increased is an understatement. The conclusion, where 'the Muse, like *Jove's* Eagle, after a sudden stoop at ignoble game, soareth again to the skies', is in 1728 almost the only passage which deals with subjects other than literature and the book-trade.[3] Such strokes of moral or political satire as there are owe their presence to some chance connexion with writing or writers. There is hardly more claim to a high moral purpose than in *MacFlecknoe*. 'This poem', as Pope wrote to Swift, 'will rid me of these insects.'[4]

---

[1] 'By failing to make Cibber his hero in 1728', comments the Twickenham editor (p. xxxvi n.), 'Pope missed a fine chance of anticipating history. To have called to the throne of Dullness the very man who in 1730 was to be given the laurel would have been a pretty irony.' But it seems likely that Pope *was* trying to anticipate history. For Theobald, no less than Cibber, wished to succeed Eusden, and apparently came near to fulfilling his ambition. (Ibid., p. xlvii.)

Although it was as a scholar that Theobald had given personal offence to Pope, at least as much emphasis is placed on his being a bad writer (he wrote plays, poems, and even began a translation of Homer, as well as having 'been concerned in the Journals') as on his pedantry. The distinction between different classes of writing was less regarded in Pope's time than today. Just as Pope tended to regard journalism as literature—bad literature—so he often regarded scholars as dull writers. He did not take it for granted, as we usually do, that journalists should write badly and scholars dully.

[2] Spence, p. 296. The whole stanza was actually written at the head of one of the manuscripts of the poem. The word 'clownish' no doubt seemed unsuitable.

[3] Note to III. 337, &c.   [4] E.-C. vii. 124.

II

The last Book of *The Dunciad* of 1728 concludes with a prophecy made by the ghost of Settle: 'First the nation shall be overrun with farces, opera's, shows; and the throne of Dulness advanced over both the Theatres: Then . . . her sons shall preside in the seats of arts and sciences, till in conclusion all shall return to their original Chaos: A scene, of which the present Action of the Dunciad is but a Type or Foretaste, giving a Glimpse or *Pisgah-sight* of the promis'd Fulness of her Glory.'[1] Whether or not Pope had from the first a notion of continuing *The Dunciad*, as he hints in this Argument, he published nothing for more than a decade; it was not until 1742 that there appeared *The New Dunciad*, in which the poet sets out 'to declare the *Completion* of the *Prophecies* mention'd at the end of the former [Book]'.[2]

'This Book may properly be distinguished from the former', a note pointed out, 'by the Name of the GREATER DUNCIAD, not so indeed in Size, but in Subject.' The poet makes a new and solemn invocation. The structure of the Book is a parody of an Oxford degree ceremony.[3] Dulness mounts her throne. Among the captives all around are not only Wit and Rhetoric, but also Science, Logic, and Morality. This indicates the wider scope of the new Book. All her subjects are summoned: they include the flatterers of dulness in great men, bad judges, and bad patrons, as well as bad writers. After a speech in which Dulness speaks in favour of a pedantic, authoritarian reign a horde of neo-Aristotelians appears, headed by Busby. He praises pedantry in a manner which recalls *The Praise of Folly*. He is followed by fops returned from the 'Grand Tour', idlers, cheating antiquarians, and 'Virtuosos'. Dulness praises them all. Atheistical

---

[1] Argument to Book III, *ad fin.*

[2] Argument to *The New Dunciad*.

[3] Pope was angry at the refusal of Oxford to confer on Warburton the degree of D.D., after several members of the University had raised his hopes of it (*E.-C.* viii. 508). Out of sympathy for his friend Pope refused any suggestion of an honorary degree for himself. 'I will die before I receive one . . ., at a place where there remains any scruple of bestowing one on you.' (*E.-C.* ix. 217, repeated on 219.)

philosophers next appear, and the merits of modern education are ironically praised. The Book draws to an end
with the ministrations of the High Priest of Dulness and
the awarding of degrees. The speech in which Dulness is
giving advice to the new graduates is brought to an end by
a tremendous yawn which spreads across the world and sends
everyone to sleep. Sense, Shame, Right, and Wrong lose
consciousness in the general torpor, and 'Universal Darkness
buries All'.

Martinus Scriblerus had claimed that the earlier Book III
'if well consider'd, seemeth to embrace the whole world'.[1]
Although that was an unjustifiable claim in 1729, it might
be made with more justice of *The New Dunciad*. In this
new poem, in which Theobald is not even mentioned, Pope
passes from Dulness in literature to Dulness in general.
Simultaneously the satire becomes rather less personal in
emphasis. Applied to this Book, the remark that 'the *Poem
was not made for these Authors, but these Authors for the Poem*'[2]
has some plausibility. The conclusion is now all-embracing
in its pessimism:

> *Religion* blushing veils her sacred fires,
> And unawares *Morality* expires.
> Nor *public* Flame, nor *private*, dares to shine;
> Nor *human* Spark is left, nor Glimpse *divine!*
> Lo! thy dread Empire, CHAOS! is restor'd;
> Light dies before thy uncreating word.[3]

Dulness is here the foe not only of Science and Taste but of
'all Obligations, divine, civil, moral, or rational'.[4] Pope has
assumed the robes of a prophet and a moralist, and is looking
back to Shakespeare's vision of Chaos and the profoundly
conservative 'world picture' of the Elizabethans and the
Middle Ages.

The New Dunciad reflects the increased interest that Pope
took in politics in the later years of his life. The primarily

---

[1] *Martinus Scriblerus of the Poem* (p. 51).
[2] *Preface prefix'd to the five imperfect Editions of the Dunciad* . . . (p. 205, Pope's italics).
[3] ll. 649–54.   [4] Argument to *The New Dunciad*.

literary scope of the satire in its first form is emphasized by the fact that it was presented by Walpole to the King; but by the time *The New Dunciad* was published Pope's sympathies were definitely and strongly with the Opposition. A writer before all else, Pope was repelled by the confusion of literary merit and political 'loyalty' encouraged by 'Bob, the poet's foe',[1] and felt a fastidious hatred for men like Concanen and Henley who prostituted such abilities as they had for the sake of the scamped and ungracious support of the Government. It is not surprising that he turned from satirizing bad writers to make a pessimistic survey of the whole intellectual and moral milieu in which they flourished.

But Pope's interest in politics was not the only reason for the shift in direction marked by *The New Dunciad*. Swift had made long visits to England in 1726 and 1727, staying with him on each occasion; and the poem on which Pope was working during both visits bears the marks of Swift's influence on every page. It was fittingly dedicated to him. 'Do you care I should say anything further how much that poem is yours?', Pope asked, 'since certainly without you it had never been. Would to God we were together for the rest of our lives! The whole weight of scribblers would just serve to find us amusement, and not more.'[2] But after 1727 Pope and Swift never met again, and latterly Swift was unable even to correspond. His influence was succeeded by that of Bolingbroke and Warburton. It was Warburton, whom Pope first met in 1740, who suggested the addition of a new Book, urging 'that it was a pity so fine a poem as the *Dunciad*, should remain disgraced by the meanness of its subject; and that he ought to raise and ennoble it by pointing his satire against minute philosophers and free-thinkers'.[3] With Warburton 'the plan of the fourth book' was 'concerted'.[4] Pope was not a weathercock, to be blown this way or that as the influence of one friend or another prevailed. But the different influences of Swift and Warburton drew out

---

[1] Swift, *An Epistle to Mr. Gay* (1731).   [2] *E.-C.* vii. 139.
[3] Ruffhead, *Life of Alexander Pope* (1769), p. 391.   [4] *E.-C.* ix. 222 n.

different traits of his own personality. As Swift's influence had encouraged his flair for direct lampooning and the invention of ludicrous incidents, so Warburton's, following on that of Bolingbroke, confirmed in him the ambition of becoming the poetic mentor of his age.

Indeed the breakdown of Pope's ambitious plans for the *Essay on Man* was the most important factor of all in the genesis of *The New Dunciad*. He had intended to write four epistles, dealing with the right application of human reason and knowledge, 'which naturally follow the Essay on Man';[1] the last of these was to 'conclude with a satire against the misapplication of [human reason and "science"], exemplified by pictures, characters, and examples'. The decision not to complete this plan left Pope with material too good to jettison. Always the most economical of poets, he devised the new Book partly as a repository for stray passages. So it happened that 200 lines 'first designed for an Epistle on Education, as part of my essay-scheme'[2] became part of *The New Dunciad*. The same use was found for other fragments.[3]

III

Pope was not content to leave *The New Dunciad* as a supplement to the earlier version in three Books. In 1743 he published *The Dunciad, In Four Books*, in which *The New Dunciad*, as Book IV, follows a revised version of the first three Books.

To give the poem what unity he could, and to prepare for the final Book, Pope inserted strokes of political and moral satire into the preceding Books. The new passages on 'the Gazetteers' and venal priests are not primarily literary in their bearing.[4] The King is now directly satirized.[5]

---

[1] *E.-C.* vii. 341.   [2] Spence, p. 289; ll. 135–336 of Book IV.
[3] On Pope's method of composition see an essay already referred to, George Sherburn's 'Pope at Work', in *Essays on the Eighteenth Century presented to David Nichol Smith*.
[4] II. 305 et seq.; II. 323 et seq.   [5] Particularly at I. 311 et seq.

As part of the general process of bringing the satire up to date fresh dunces were frequently substituted for old, 'in like manner as when the old boughs wither, we thrust new ones into a chimney';[1] and occasionally Pope took the opportunity of pillorying a dunce with more definite political connexions than his predecessor, as in his substitution of Arnall for Welsted.[2]

This is particularly true of the principal change, the substitution of Cibber for Theobald as hero of the poem. It is unlikely that Pope needed much urging from Warburton to make a change: when Cibber gave him mortal offence he must quickly have realized that he had a perfect hero for the revised poem. Cibber had a good deal in common with Boswell (including a small share of Boswell's genius), and was precisely the sort of person who is most readily ridiculed. His autobiography, which had recently been published, seemed highly ridiculous to an age unused to that form.[3] But it was his strong Whig sympathies which must have confirmed Pope's choice. Although in both versions of the poem there is a couplet suggesting that it is a sign of Dulness to be a supporter of either party,[4] it would have conflicted with the general tendency of the 1743 *Dunciad* to have retained the lines in which Theobald decided to write in the Tory interest. Instead Cibber apostrophizes Dulness in these words:

> Hold—to the Minister I more incline;
> To serve his cause, O Queen! is serving thine.[5]

[1] *Preface prefix'd to the five imperfect Editions of the Dunciad* ... (p. 206).

[2] (B) II. 315 et seq., (A) II. 293 et seq.

[3] I. 217-24:
> What then remains? Ourself. Still, still remain
> Cibberian forehead, and Cibberian brain ...

refer to Cibber's *Apology for the Life of Mr. Colley Cibber, Comedian* (1740).

For the theme of self-love cf. *The Memoirs of Martinus Scriblerus*, ch. xi : 'Whom does he generally talk of? Himself, quoth the aunt.—Whose wit and breeding does he most commend? His own (quoth the aunt).—Whom does he write letters to? Himself.—Whom does he dream of? All the dreams I ever heard were of himself.—Whom is he ogling yonder? Himself in his looking-glass.'

[4] III. 283-6 in (A), shifted (with a slight change) to I. 205-8 in (B).

[5] I. 213-14.

The fact that Cibber was now Poet Laureate fitted in well; for as the author of *A Blast upon Bays* remarked, 'To be the titular Monarch of Wit, and receive a Salary in that Capacity; must it not make Folly the more egregious, where it was before remarkable?'[1]

One alteration made in 1743 which is even more important from a formal point of view than the substitution of Cibber for Theobald is a change in the subject proposed in the opening lines of the poem. What the poet sets out to describe is no longer the manner in which one dunce succeeded another on the throne of Dulness, but the activities of the 'Mighty Mother' herself (together with those of her son):

> Say how the Goddess bade Britannia sleep,
> And pour'd her Spirit o'er the land and deep.[2]

In 1728 Theobald was the protagonist of the poem, Dulness merely a piece of 'machinery' enhancing the mock solemnity of the action and parodying the supernatural agents of the epic. In 1743, as Warburton pointed out, 'the *Mother*, and not the *Son*, is the principal Agent of this Poem. . . . The main action . . . being by no means the Coronation of the Laureate, which is performed in the very first book, but the Restoration of the Empire of Dulness in Britain, which is not accomplished 'till the last.'[3]

Those who claim that the *Dunciad* of 1743 is a unified poem on a profound subject must insist on the comprehensiveness of the term Dulness. Warburton·was emphatic about it. 'Dulness here is not to be taken contractedly for mere Stupidity', he wrote in his note on line 15, 'but in the enlarged sense of the word, for all Slowness of Apprehension, Shortness of Sight, or imperfect Sense of things. . . . A ruling principle not inert, but turning topsy-turvy the Understanding, and inducing an Anarchy or confused State of Mind.' Only when this is understood will it be appreciated

---

[1] (1742), p. 6. Quoted by Root, p. 222.   [2] I. 7–8.
[3] Note to l. 1. The Twickenham editor's comment—'Apparently an attempt by Warburton to answer a frequent criticism of the *Dunciad*, viz. that the hero *did* nothing'—contains only part of the truth: the main reason for the note was the shift of intention between 1728 and 1743.

that while 'some have complained [that Pope] chuses too mean a subject, and imagined he employs himself, like Domitian, in killing flies . . . those who have the true key will find he sports with nobler quarry, and embraces a larger compass; or (as one saith, on a like occasion)

> Will see his Work, like Jacob's ladder, rise,
> Its foot in dirt, its head amid the skies.'[1]

Yet in spite of the comprehensiveness of the term Dulness the *Dunciad* of 1743 is not a unified whole. On account of the difference of scope and intention between the two works it is very doubtful whether it would have been possible by any method to weld the original three Books and *The New Dunciad* into a unity. There is little evidence that Pope made any determined effort to do so. The 1743 text of Books I–III does not differ very greatly from that of 1728.[2] As always happened when Pope revised a poem, passages were suppressed, transposed and added, while new dunces took the place of old. But it remains almost as true in 1743 as before that while the last Book has a wide scope and a serious moral

---

[1] In giving Dulness this wide connotation Pope had the example of 'honest Erasmus', whose 'Folly' embraces every aspect of human activity.

As early as 1707, moreover, Pope had been closely concerned with the writing of a 'poem on Dulness'. On the 20th November of that year he wrote to Wycherley about his revision of the latter's poem. 'The poem is now divided into four parts. . . . The first contains the praise of Dulness, and shows how upon several suppositions it passes for, 1. religion; 2. philosophy; 3. example; 4. wit; and 5. the cause of wit, and the end of it. The second part contains the advantages of Dulness; 1st, in business; and 2dly, at court, where the similitudes of the bias of a bowl, and the weights of a clock, are directly tending to illustrate the advantages of Dulness. . . . The third contains the happiness of Dulness in all stations, and shows in a great many particulars that it is so fortunate as to be esteemed some good quality or other in all sorts of people; that it is thought quiet, sense, caution, policy, prudence, majesty, valour, circumspection, honesty, &c. The fourth part I have wholly added, as a climax which sums up all the praise, advantage, and happiness of Dulness in a few words, and strengthens them by the opposition of the disgrace, disadvantage, and unhappiness of wit, with which it concludes.' (*E.-C.* vi. 31–32.)

The general plan of Wycherley's poem, so thoroughly remodelled by himself, obviously remained in Pope's mind and influenced him when he came to write his own 'poem on Dulness'—particularly *The New Dunciad*. Verbal echoes may even be found. The similes from the bias of a bowl and the weights of a clock (for the earlier history of the latter see p. 130, n. 3, below) are used with effect at (B) I, 181–4.

This suggests a slight modification of Courthope's view that the metaphysical part of *The New Dunciad* was 'largely inspired by Warburton'. (*E.-C.* v. 337.)

[2] From Cibber himself onwards, critics have noted Pope's failure to adapt the satirical portrait of Theobald in Book I to Cibber's very different, and quite un-antiquarian, character.

purpose, the first three Books are primarily concerned with Dulness in literature and are largely retaliatory in intention. The result, as Warton pointed out, is 'a marvellous mixture and jumble of images and sentiments, Pantomime and Philosophy, Journals and Moral evidence, Fleet-ditch and the High Priori road, *Curl* and *Clarke*. . . .'[1] The poet who began as a wit attacking bad writers ends by trying to persuade us that he is a righteous satirist lashing the follies of an age. He is both. But a 'Burlesque Heroick on Writers, & ye modern Diversions of the Town'[2] could not be changed into a comprehensive Satire on the Age in such a manner.

I V

The idiom in which *The Dunciad* is written varies in a manner which reflects the diversity of its origins. In a general sense it is a mock-heroic poem. Following the example of *MacFlecknoe* Pope turns to satiric account many of the characteristics of the epic, such as the proposition of the subject, the invocation, the division into Books, the episode of the 'heroic Games', 'machinery', and the prophecy by a ghost with which Book III concludes. The style which the reader expects, therefore, is something comparable to the style of *MacFlecknoe*: an elevated 'heroic' idiom used for the purpose of ridicule.

In many parts of the poem that is what one finds. In the opening lines, for example—

> The Mighty Mother, and her Son who brings
> The Smithfield Muses to the ear of Kings,
> I sing . . .[3]

—the idiom is heroic, reduced to the mock-heroic by the word 'Smithfield', just as the elevated opening of *Mac-Flecknoe* is brought to earth by the unheroic 'Fleckno'. The

[1] *Essay*, ii. 374.
[2] Edward Young's description of the three-book version in a letter to Thomas Tickell. (R. E. Tickell, *Thomas Tickell and the Eighteenth Century Poets* (1931), p. 143—cited in the Twickenham edition, p. xvii.)
[3] All quotations in this section are from the (B) text.

same combination of heroic 'numbers' with an elevated diction and ordering of the words may be found at many points, in the second paragraph of the poem, for example:

> In eldest time, e'er mortals writ or read,
> E'er Pallas issu'd from the Thund'rer's head,
> Dulness o'er all possess'd her ancient right,
> Daughter of Chaos and eternal Night

or slightly later (in particularly obvious parody of Dryden's *Virgil*):

> And thrice he lifted high the Birth-day brand,
> And thrice he dropt it from his quiv'ring hand;
> Then lights the structure, with averted eyes:
> The rowling smokes involve the sacrifice.[1]

Here the repetition, the sentence-structure, and the choice of words (not least the Latin 'averted' and 'involve') all proclaim the idiom as heroic; and the fact that it is not the cremation of a hero that is being described, but Cibber's burning of his own bad plays and poems, turns the effect to the mock-heroic. Similarly Pope's imagery often parodies that of the epic:

> Tears gush'd again, as from pale Priam's eyes
> When the last blaze sent Ilion to the skies.[2]

This is a heroic comparison rendered mock-heroic by its application to Cibber. Pope also uses a number of images which parody the Homeric simile:

> As when the long-ear'd milky mothers wait
> At some sick miser's triple-bolted gate,
> For their defrauded, absent foals they make
> A moan so loud, that all the guild awake;
> Sore sighs Sir Gilbert.[3]

Imagery of this sort, which is to be expected in a mock-heroic poem, is plentiful.

Yet neither in the version of 1728 nor in that of 1743 is

---

[1] I. 245–8.—The Twickenham editor points out the parody of Dryden's *Æneid*, viii. 141.
[2] I. 255–6.   [3] II. 247–51.

the idiom of *The Dunciad* consistently mock-heroic. Many passages are much lower in style than is strictly appropriate. In the following lines from Bentley's speech in Book IV there is nothing, after the first couplet, to mark the style as heroic:

> Mistress! dismiss that rabble from your throne:
> Avaunt—is Aristarchus yet unknown?
> Thy mighty Scholiast, whose unweary'd pains
> Made Horace dull, and humbled Milton's strains.
> Turn what they will to Verse, their toil is vain,
> Critics like me shall make it Prose again.
> Roman and Greek Grammarians! know your Better:
> Author of something yet more great than Letter;
> While tow'ring o'er your Alphabet, like Saul,
> Stands our Digamma, and o'er-tops them all.
> 'Tis true, on Words is still our whole debate,
> Disputes of *Me* or *Te*, of *aut* or *at*,
> To sound or sink in *cano*, O or A,
> Or give up Cicero to C or K.
> Let Freind affect to speak as Terence spoke,
> And Alsop never but like Horace joke:
> For me, what Virgil, Pliny may deny,
> Manilius or Solinus shall supply:
> For Attic Phrase in Plato let them seek,
> I poach in Suidas for unlicens'd Greek.[1]

These lines are excellent satire, but they would be perfectly appropriate in the middle of one of the *Imitations of Horace*.

One reason for the mixture of styles in *The Dunciad* is manifestly the fact that passages now incorporated in it were written at various times and with various purposes. The lines just quoted, for example, were originally intended to form part of a satiric epistle.[2] But only some of the variations of idiom can be explained in this way. There are many passages in *The Dunciad* which do not appear to have been written for any other poem but where 'the numbers of heroic poetry' are completely absent, and one finds instead the less musical

---

[1] IV. 209–28.   [2] See p. 122, above.

movement of epistolary verse. Feminine rhymes, which are not characteristic of elevated verse, are fairly common:

> From drawing rooms, from colleges, from garrets,
> On horse, on foot, in hacks, and gilded chariots.[1]

Sometimes the effect is to lower the style to near the level of burlesque:

> Yet lo! in me what authors have to brag on!
> Reduc'd at last to hiss in my own dragon.[2]

And although the images of ironical aggrandizement particularly associated with the mock-heroic form are frequent in *The Dunciad*, Pope also makes use of 'low' imagery in a manner appropriate rather to the more direct species of satire:

> No meagre, muse-rid mope, adust and thin,
> In a dun night-gown of his own loose skin;
> But such a bulk as no twelve bards could raise,
> Twelve starv'ling bards of these degen'rate days.
> All as a partridge plump, full-fed, and fair,
> She form'd this image of well-body'd air;
> With pert flat eyes she window'd well its head;
> A brain of feathers, and a heart of lead;
> And empty words she gave, and sounding strain,
> But senseless, lifeless! idol void and vain![3]

The images here are indeed 'wonderfully short and thick-sown';[4] but in spite of the ironical compliment with which the description begins there is little that is mock-heroic in the idiom. Whereas Dryden in *MacFlecknoe* allowed himself one or two passages consisting of a string of directly denigratory images (a technique not strictly mock-heroic, as such imagery has no place in a heroic poem), the imagery of *The Rape of the Lock* is modelled strictly on that of the epic: metaphors and similes are introduced sparingly, always at structurally important places where some 'heightening' of style is called for. In *The Dunciad*, on the other hand, Pope

---

[1] II. 23–24.   [2] III. 285–6.
[3] II. 37–46.
[4] *Testimonies of Authors* (p. 42 in the Twickenham edition).

reverted to the use of denigrating imagery much more frequently than Dryden had done:

> O thou! of Bus'ness the directing soul!
> To this our head like byass to the bowl,
> Which, as more pond'rous, made its aim more true,
> Obliquely wadling to the mark in view:
> O! ever gracious to perplex'd mankind,
> Still spread a healing mist before the mind;
> And lest we err by Wit's wild dancing light,
> Secure us kindly in our native night.
> Or, if to Wit a coxcomb make pretence,
> Guard the sure barrier between that and Sense;
> Or quite unravel all the reas'ning thread,
> And hang some curious cobweb in its stead!
> As, forc'd from wind-guns, lead itself can fly,
> And pond'rous slugs cut swiftly thro the sky;
> As clocks to weight their nimble motion owe,
> The wheels above urg'd by the load below:
> Me Emptiness, and Dulness could inspire,
> And were my Elasticity, and Fire.[1]

In *The Art of Sinking* Pope recommends that the aspirant to
bad heroic poetry should 'be able, on the appearance of any
Object, to furnish his Imagination with Ideas infinitely below
it. . . . His Eyes should be like unto the wrong end of a Perspective Glass, by which all the Objects of Nature are less-
en'd.'[2]   The method here ironically recommended to the
heroic poet is precisely that which Pope himself uses in such
satire as this.[3] For all his mock-heroic framework, Pope has

---

[1] I. 169–86.   [2] Ch. v.

[3] The image of a clock in the lines just quoted has an interesting history. Pope first used
it in his juvenile epic, *Alcander* (Spence, pp. 277–8). But later he seems to have felt that it was
a 'low' image, more suitable for satire, for he transferred it to his early satire *To the Author
of a Poem, intitled 'Successio'* (ll. 3–4). From there, much changed, it was transferred—with the
image of a bullet (ll. 17–18)—to *The Dunciad*.

This is not the only passage in *The Dunciad* where Pope uses his own bad verse in a 'high'
style for the purposes of satire. The couplet on the circulation of the blood (III. 55–56), for
example, has the same origin (Spence, p. 25). And since 'there was an under-water scene in
the first book' (Spence, p. 276), it is not unlikely that touches in the diving-competition in
Book II also come from the early poem. Lines 333–6 may be an example:

> How young Lutetia, softer than the down,
> Nigrina black, and Merdamante brown,

worked his way right back into the current of traditional vernacular satire.

In the treatment of Cibber, and even more in that of the minor dunces, direct satire predominates over the mock-heroic. When the dunces are portrayed in action there are mock-heroic touches, but very often they are merely described, and the style used for the descriptions is that of the satirical 'character'. Unless a satirical 'character' is ironical it tends to destroy the mock-heroic illusion before it has a chance to establish itself. And whereas in *The Rape of the Lock* Sir Plume is the only character who is imaginatively killed in this way, in *The Dunciad* most of the characters are so treated. Pope is not prepared to undergo the willing suspension of contempt by which alone the mock-heroic poet performs his task. In *The Dunciad* no compelling world of the imagination is born, as it is in *The Rape of the Lock*. One listens in vain for the large laughter of *MacFlecknoe*.

But it is not only the presence of passages in a middle or low style that distinguishes *The Dunciad* from a pure mock-heroic poem. It also contains passages as elevated in their idiom as anything that Pope wrote. A good example is the following, from Book III:

> How little, mark! that portion of the ball,
> Where, faint at best, the beams of Science fall:
> Soon as they dawn, from Hyperborean skies
> Embody'd dark, what clouds of Vandals rise!
> Lo! where Mæotis sleeps, and hardly flows
> The freezing Tanais thro' a waste of snows,
> The North by myriads pours her mighty sons,
> Great nurse of Goths, of Alans, and of Huns![1]

There is nothing mock-heroic about these lines, in which Pope gives expression to the profound melancholy of a

Vy'd for his love in jetty bow'rs below,
As Hylas fair was ravish'd long ago.

The names of the nymphs have no doubt been changed; but the lines retain a curious Romantic overtone.

[1] III. 83–90.

Christian humanist. The style is closer to that of *The Vanity of Human Wishes* than that of any other poem dealt with in this volume. It is a passage we should expect to find rather in an epic or a didactic poem than in a mock-heroic composition.

The fact that this passage comes from Book III, and was printed (in a slightly different form) in the 1728 version, proves that it would be false to attribute the appearance of an elevated idiom in *The Dunciad* simply to Pope's change of plan. Yet, as we should expect, elevated passages are more noticeable in Book IV than elsewhere:

> Yet, yet a moment, one dim Ray of Light
> Indulge, dread Chaos, and eternal Night!
> Of darkness visible so much be lent,
> As half to shew, half veil the deep Intent.
> Ye Pow'rs! whose Mysteries restor'd I sing,
> To whom Time bears me on his rapid wing,
> Suspend a while your Force inertly strong,
> Then take at once the Poet and the Song.[1]

The verbal echo in 'darkness visible' is hardly necessary to remind the reader that Pope had Milton in mind as he wrote these lines:[2] there is an unmistakable reminiscence of the Invocation to Light at the beginning of Book III of *Paradise Lost*. It would be a complete mistake to think of such a passage simply as a 'parody', in any sense suggesting that the meaning is other than serious. Pope is gathering all his powers for the conclusion of a poem with profoundly important implications. Like other 'literary' poets, notably Virgil and Milton himself, Pope is the more given to allusions to earlier poetry the more surely he is finding his own truest inspiration. In this great opening, which it would be quite unhelpful to classify as 'satiric', allusions to earlier heroic poets are drawn into the orbit of his inspiration and help him to rise to a consummate passage of sublime poetry. Like the great lines

---

[1] IV. 1–8.   [2] *Paradise Lost*, I. 63.

at the end of the poem,[1] this passage is an example of Pope's heroic style which cannot be surpassed by anything in his poems in more professedly elevated kinds.

It is primarily at such key-points in *The Dunciad* as the openings of the Books, the introductions of speeches, and the formal descriptions that the idiom is unmistakably mock-heroic. In other parts of the poem Pope frequently makes use of mock-heroic touches; but he has also many passages which are much closer to the lower and more direct species of satire, and a number of sublime passages. It was this mixture of styles that Warton was censuring when he called *The Dunciad* 'one of the most motley compositions . . . in the works of so exact a writer'.[2]

That a modern critic should agree with Warton may seem absurd. Granted that many passages in *The Dunciad* have nothing mock-heroic about them (it may be argued), and granted that many might be transferred to one of the *Moral Essays* without the change being noticed, this is not necessarily an adverse criticism. In fact, however, the principle of decorum is not merely a historical curiosity: in some form it is a permanent requirement of all good poetry. It is partly to its sure observance of decorum that the superiority of *The Rape of the Lock* is to be attributed. With *The Dunciad*, on the other hand, the reader may be excused for forgetting

---

[1] Spence may have influenced the conclusion of *The Dunciad*. In the second part of his *Essay on Pope's Odyssey*, with reference to Book xx. 429–30—

> Nor gives the Sun his golden Orb to roll,
> But universal night usurps the pole!

—Antiphaus observes that he admires the 'Orientalism', 'that *Eastern way of expressing Revolutions in Government, by a Confusion or Extinction of Light in the Heavens*' (pp. 56–57, Spence's italics). He mentions similar examples from the Bible.

Pope was pleased with the first part of the *Essay*, which appeared about the beginning of June 1726, and made Spence's acquaintance shortly afterwards. He saw the second part before it was published, the following year, and may have taken a hint from this passage.

[2] *Essay*, ii. 374. The author of an anonymous *Criticism on the Elegy Written in a Country Church-Yard* (1783) severely censures the 'confusion and inconsequence . . . which was introduced into the Dunciad, when Pope, at the instigation of Warburton, changed the hero of that piece; and which, the poet and his Mentor, who kept botching it during the whole of their lives, were not able to remove; though the labour of Procrustes was doubled, and both the tortured and instruments of torture were racked to produce accommodation' (ed. of 1810, pp. 22–23).

about the mock-heroic basis for long passages at a time; as a result the satiric effect of the whole poem is seriously impoverished. Although *The Dunciad* contains some of Pope's finest poetry—Book IV was his own 'favourite work'[1]—Warton was right in diagnosing a fatal weakness: what the eighteenth century called a lack of unity and decorum: what we may recognize more readily if we call it a fundamental uncertainty about the subject of the poem, a fatal indefiniteness of purpose. In *The Rape of the Lock* Pope turned to consummate use the discovery made by Dryden in *MacFlecknoe*: the tremendous gain resulting from a consistent following-out of the mock-heroic idea. In *The Dunciad* he turned his back on it.

[1] Ruffhead, p. 394.

VIII

'TRAGICAL SATIRE': *THE VANITY OF HUMAN WISHES*

A Satyr as it was borne out of a Tragedy, *so ought to resemble his parentage, to strike high, and adventure dangerously at the most eminent vices among the greatest persons.*   MILTON[1]

As Edward Young pointed out, the term 'satire' is not 'unapplicable to graver compositions. Ethics, Heathen and Christian, and the Scriptures themselves, are, in a great measure, a satire on the weakness and iniquity of men.'[2] *The Vanity of Human Wishes*, 'a poem of the moral and didactic species',[3] is in many ways more reminiscent of the Book of Job, of Prior's *Solomon*[4] or Johnson's own *Rasselas*, than of *Hudibras* and *The Rape of the Lock*, *MacFlecknoe* and the *Epistle to Arbuthnot*. It is a discourse without a plot, a pessimistic survey of human life in which the poet enforces his lesson with a series of *exempla* in the manner of a preacher. Like its model it ends with the short didactic coda conventional in the classical *satura*, which was commonly made up of a major part which attacks vice, and a minor part in which virtue is recommended.[5]

It is the prominence of the element of attack which makes *The Vanity of Human Wishes*, like its Juvenalian original, a satire in the English sense of the word. What distinguishes it from the *Essay on Man*, for example—a poem with which it has marked similarities—is that it takes its tone from its primary rhetorical function of 'diminishing' human life. While several of the finest passages in the *Essay on Man* have

---

[1] *An Apology, &c.*, Sect. 6, in the *Works*, Columbia edition (1931–40), III. i, p. 329.

[2] Preface to *Love of Fame, the Universal Passion*, in *Works* (1774), i. 65.

[3] Joseph Warton in H. J. Todd's edition of Dryden's *Poetical Works* (1811), iv. 367 n.

[4] In 'The "Choice of Life" in Johnson and Matthew Prior' (*J.E.G.P.*, Oct. 1950) I have suggested that the conception and style of *The Vanity of Human Wishes* and *Rasselas* owe a debt to *Solomon*, a poem—as Johnson remarked in his *Life of Prior*—containing 'many passages ... from which the poet may learn to write, and the philosopher to reason' (*Lives*, ii. 207).

[5] See an article already cited, 'The Structural Design of the Formal Verse Satire', by Mary Claire Randolph, *P.Q.*, Oct. 1942.

this function,[1] Pope's main intention is to survey human life and make sense of it. Johnson does not aim at explanation: his concern, like Juvenal's, is to underline the insecurity of man's existence and the futility of selfish ambitions. This intention gives *The Vanity of Human Wishes* its characteristic accent.

In Juvenal Johnson found a perfect model. The affinity of Juvenal's Stoicism with certain aspects of Christianity was early recognized by the Church. The Tenth Satire, on which Johnson's poem is founded, was particularly popular. 'This Divine Satyr', as Dryden called it,[2] is the first of the more reflective satires which contrast so strongly with those which go before that a German scholar was driven to the theory that there were two Juvenals.[3] Throughout the Middle Ages it furnished preachers with topics and examples, and it continued to be used in this way in the seventeenth and eighteenth centuries. Dryden mentions that it was recommended, along with the satires of Persius, in a pastoral letter written by the Bishop of Salisbury, 'to the serious perusal and practice of the divines in his diocese, as the best commonplaces for their sermons, [and] as the store-houses and magazines of moral virtues, from whence they may draw out, as they have occasion, all manner of assistance for the accomplishment of a virtuous life'.[4]

It was not only the similarity between Juvenal's ethical position and his own that appealed to Johnson, as to so many Christians before him. He was impressed also by Juvenal's magnificent rhetoric. Juvenal was a professional pleader for many years before he began to write satire, and his poems owe a considerable debt to the rhetorical theory of his time.[5] In his work Johnson found at once a sombre reading of life which had much in common with his own and an object-lesson in the art of impressing what he had to say on the minds of his readers.

[1] Notably the lines inspired by Pascal, Epistle ii, ll. 3–18.

[2] 'Argument' to his translation.

[3] Ribbeck, *Der echte und der unechte Juvenal* (1865). This theory has been abandoned.

[4] *Essays*, ii. 76. The Bishop of Salisbury was the historian, Gilbert Burnet.

[5] See R. J. E. Tiddy's 'Satura and Satire', in *English Literature and the Classics*, collected by G. S. Gordon (Oxford, 1912), p. 219.

When Joseph Warton remarked that Johnson 'certainly would not have succeeded so well if he had ever attempted to imitate Horace',[1] he had in mind not only the differences between the work of the two great Latin satirists which are most evident to the modern reader, but also the interpretations of their work made current by the editions and commentaries of the scholars of the Renaissance. As has been mentioned earlier, the editors of Horace and Juvenal did not scruple to deduce from the works of the satirist of their choice universal rules of satire. Juvenal's admirers held that Horace's satires were written in a style too low for the true dignity of satire, while Vossius and others insisted that '*Horatian* Satire is the only true one; and the Writings of *Juvenal* and *Persius* have no Pretence to that Title'.[2] From this controversy was born the theory that there were two different species of satire, each legitimate and each governed by its own rules. 'The Comick Satirist', Dennis remarked, 'who owes no small Part of his Excellence to his Experience, that is, to the Knowledge of the Conversation and Manners of the Men of the World, [will] be in all likelihood more agreeable to the discerning Part of a Court, and a great Capital'; while 'the Tragick Satire, which like Tragedy fetches its Notions from Philosophy and from common Sense, [will] be in all probability more acceptable to Universities and Cloisters, and all those Recluse and Contemplative Men, who pass most of their Time in their Closets, all which Persons are suppos'd to have Philosophy from Study, and common Sense from Nature'.[3] This difference of tone, which resulted in a difference of style, is the heart of the distinction.[4] And as Horace's man-of-the-world manner, casual,

---

[1] Todd's edition of Dryden's *Poetical Works*, iv. 368 n.

[2] Summarized by Trapp, p. 227.

[3] *To Matthew Prior, Esq; Upon the Roman Satirists* (1721), Hooker, ii. 219. Cf. Garrick's remark, 'When Johnson lived much with the Herveys, and saw a good deal of what was passing in life, he wrote his "London", which is lively and easy. When he became more retired, he gave us his "Vanity of Human Wishes", which is as hard as Greek. . . .' Boswell's *Life*, ed. Hill–Powell, i (1934), 194.

[4] John Brown's verse *Essay on Satire* (1745, reprinted in Warburton's *Pope*, 1751, vol. iii), contrasts the manners of Horace and Juvenal in the usual way (particularly Pt. II, ll. 293–314). Johnson no doubt knew this poem.

urbane, insinuating, confidential, was a perfect model for Pope; so the declamatory grandeur of Juvenal, with its tone of a dignified public utterance, austere, exacting, sternly censorious, afforded Johnson the precedent and the example that he required. 'He could not rally', as Dryden said of Juvenal, 'but he could declaim; and as his provocations were great, he has revenged them tragically.'[1]

The personal quality of the *Imitations of Horace* contrasts with the impersonality of *The Vanity of Human Wishes*. In Pope's epistolary satires, as in Horace, autobiography is a prominent element: in Johnson's great poem, as in the Tenth Satire of Juvenal, it is completely lacking. While Pope chats wittily with his friends, rising only occasionally, and with the most carefully managed of transitions, to a more elevated tone, Johnson is in the pulpit throughout, addressing a congregation. Pope chooses for his examples living men and women, often the objects of strong personal animosity. Johnson, aiming at a detachment and grandeur rivalling that of History itself, confines himself to 'the most eminent vices among the greatest persons'. Disdaining Atticus, Sporus, and Atossa he writes of Wolsey, Charles of Sweden, Galileo, and 'Persia's tyrant'.[2]

II

As the thoughts of Juvenal are 'much more elevated'[3] than those of Horace, they are fittingly expressed in a style akin to that of tragedy.[4] To gain a similar effect Johnson

[1] *Essays*, ii. 94.

[2] 'Proper *satire* is distinguished, by the generality of the reflections, from a lampoon.' Johnson's *Dictionary*.

[3] Dryden's *Essays*, ii. 85.

[4] See Vossius, quoted by Trapp, p. 229. Juvenal himself mentioned the elevation of his style:

> You think this feign'd; the Satyr in a Rage
> Struts in the Buskins of the Tragick Stage.
> Forgets his Bus'ness is to Laugh and Bite;
> And will, of Deaths, and dire Revenges Write.
> Wou'd it were all a Fable, that you Read . . . .

Satire VI, Dryden's translation, ll. 828–32.

used much more 'numerous' verse than that of the *Imitations
of Horace*, and a 'sublime and lofty'[1] diction:

> The march begins in military state,
> And nations on his eye suspended wait;
> Stern Famine guards the solitary coast,
> And Winter barricades the realms of Frost;
> He comes, not want and cold his course delay;—
> Hide, blushing Glory, hide Pultowa's day:
> The vanquish'd hero leaves his broken bands,
> And shews his miseries in distant lands;
> Condemn'd a needy supplicant to wait,
> While ladies interpose, and slaves debate.
> But did not Chance at length her error mend?
> Did no subverted empire mark his end?
> Did rival monarchs give the fatal wound?
> Or hostile millions press him to the ground?
> His fall was destin'd to a barren strand,
> A petty fortress, and a dubious hand;
> He left the name, at which the world grew pale,
> To point a moral, or adorn a tale.[2]

Dryden's remark that Juvenal's expressions are 'sonorous
and more noble'[1] than Horace's applies also to the comparison between *The Vanity of Human Wishes* and Pope's
epistolary satires.

The abstract generality of idiom noticeable in some
degree in all Johnson's writing is used with great skill to
contribute to the elevation of the style of his 'tragical satire'.
In many passages abstractions and personifications are the
key-words:

> In full-blown *dignity*, see Wolsey stand,
> *Law* in his voice, and *fortune* in his hand:
> To him *the church, the realm*, their *pow'rs* consign,
> Thro' him the rays of regal *bounty* shine,
> Turn'd by his nod the stream of *honour* flows,
> His smile alone *security* bestows:

---

[1] Dryden's *Essays*, ii. 85.

[2] ll. 205–22. Quotations are from *The Poems of Samuel Johnson*, ed. David Nichol Smith
and Edward L. McAdam (1941).

> Still to new heights his restless *wishes* tow'r,
> *Claim* leads to *claim*, and *pow'r* advances *pow'r*;
> Till *conquest* unresisted ceas'd to please,
> And *rights* submitted, left him none to seize.[1]

Such abstractions are very different from the type commonly associated with unsuccessful Augustan verse. They are the manifestation and embodiment of concentrated meaning and a weighty seriousness.

In the work of many poets there is some characteristic of style which becomes most evident when they are writing at the top of their bent. This unusual fondness for abstract personifications is Johnson's characteristic. Just as Donne's images tend to become more and more daring as his inspiration catches fire, so the better Johnson is writing the more prominent abstract personifications become. It is when he has gathered all his powers and is deploying his poetic rhetoric with supreme effect that he makes the fullest use of abstractions and personifications:

> Are these thy views? proceed, illustrious youth,
> And *virtue* guard thee to the throne of *Truth*!
> Yet should thy soul indulge the gen'rous heat,
> Till captive *Science* yields her last retreat;
> Should *Reason* guide thee with her brightest ray,
> And pour on misty *Doubt* resistless day;
> Should no false *Kindness* lure to loose delight,
> Nor *Praise* relax, nor *Difficulty* fright;
> Should tempting *Novelty* thy cell refrain,
> And *Sloth* effuse her opiate fumes in vain;
> Should *Beauty* blunt on fops her fatal dart,
> Nor claim the triumph of a letter'd heart;
> Should no Disease thy torpid veins invade,
> Nor *Melancholy's* phantoms haunt thy shade;
> Yet hope not life from *grief* or *danger* free,
> Nor think the *doom* of man revers'd for thee.[2]

---

[1] ll. 99–108. (My italics.)   [2] ll. 141–56. (My italics.)

Johnson is not a highly versatile poet. Perhaps it was the fact that he evolved this one characteristic kind of imagery, making little attempt to supplement it with any other, that determined the poetic genres in which he was to excel. Dramatic poetry demands a wide range of imagery, and derives little nutriment from abstractions. In writing *Irene* Johnson

Critics have often fallen into the danger of condemning one species of personification by contrast with another. It is the task of the critic to be empirical, judging each example as he meets it, and making no attempt to lay down universal laws for poetry. To condemn Johnson's abstract sort of personification out of hand, contrasting it (for example) with Keats's use of the figure, is as futile as it would be to condemn the prose of De Quincey by comparing it with Swift's. Just as De Quincey and Swift were aiming at different effects, and used different means to attain them, so Johnson and a Romantic poet aim, in their use of personification, at different results. It is not surprising that they use different methods. To condemn Johnson for 'failing to bring his personifications to life' (by which is usually meant failing to bring them before the mind's eye) is uncritical. That was not the sort of effect that he wished to gain.

Elevation of style is not the only result of Johnson's use of an unusually abstract idiom. An effect of philosophic generality, and a remarkable conciseness, are equally noteworthy. Johnson belonged to an age which found generalizations about human life exciting,[1] when many critics held, with Imlac, that the true poet 'must divest himself of the prejudices of his age or country; . . . must consider right and

seems to have realized that a greater than ordinary richness of imagery was called for, and to have attempted to make up for his lack of versatility by packing his lines with abstractions and personifications. This fails to bring the play to life. To such moralizing declamations as the two imitations of Juvenal, on the other hand, Johnson's species of imagery is well suited; and it is interesting to note that *The Vanity of Human Wishes*, which is by common consent the better poem, contains far more abstractions than *London*. Such an idiom is equally effective in serious occasional poems, such as the prologues (which are unusually serious) and the epitaphs. Almost as successful as the celebrated poem *On the Death of Dr. Robert Levet* is the conclusion of the epitaph on Hogarth:

> The Hand of Art here torpid lies
>   That traced th'essential form of Grace,
> Here death has clos'd the curious eyes
>   That saw the manners in the Face.

> If Genius warm thee, Reader, stay,
>   If Merit touch thee, shed a tear,
> Be Vice and Dulness far away
>   Great Hogarth's honour'd Dust is here.

Abstraction is here essential to the effect of impressive sententiousness.

[1] See Bertrand H. Bronson's 'Personification Reconsidered', *E.L.H.*, Sept. 1947.

wrong in their abstracted and invariable state; . . . must disregard present laws and opinions, and rise to general and transcendental truths, which will always be the same'.[1] The use of highly generalized figures in *The Vanity of Human Wishes* exemplifies one of the most direct ways in which the poet can give expression to his general observations. What Rymer called 'the greater force and emphasis [of] the *abstract*'[2] was thus a rhetorical effect with a philosophical basis. Further, *Worth* and *Science* are not only dignified and philosophical ways of saying *those who deserve a reward* and *men of learning*: they are also remarkably concise. Similarly in the lines

> Around his tomb let Art and Genius weep,
> But hear his death, ye blockheads, hear and sleep,[3]

Art and *Genius*, which contrast with the concrete and undignified *ye blockheads*,[4] are more concise as well as more dignified than their concrete equivalents. Such effects led Joseph Warton to remark on the 'diction remarkably close and compact'[5] of this poem.[6]

Closely connected with his preference for abstraction is Johnson's use of what may be termed 'the generic article'. Instead of *learned men* he may say *Science*: equally he may say *the knowing*. He felt this to be a gain in elevation and in philosophical generality, though not in conciseness. This use of the generalized individual for the species is very common in *The Vanity of Human Wishes*. Nothing is more characteristic than the frequency of such phrases as *the vassal . . . the lord*; *the hind*; *the needy traveller*; *the toiling statesman*;

---

[1] *Rasselas*, ch. x, ed. R. W. Chapman (1927), pp. 50–51.

[2] Spingarn, ii. 181. Cited by James Sutherland in *A Preface to Eighteenth Century Poetry* (1948), p. 169.

[3] ll. 173–4.

[4] Like 'driv'ler' (l. 318), 'blockheads' may be an attempt on Johnson's part to imitate Juvenal's habit of mixing colloquialisms with his predominantly heroic diction. This characteristic of Juvenal's was frequently remarked on by critics of the period.

[5] Todd's edition of Dryden's *Poetical Works*, iv. 368 n.

[6] Johnson's fondness for abstractions may also be regarded, like his preference for Latin for the expression of many of his most private feelings (cf. D. Nichol Smith, 'Samuel Johnson's Poems', *R.E.S.*, Jan. 1943), as a shy man's desire for a cloak.

th' insidious rival and the gaping heir; the glitt'ring eminence;
and *the plunder'd palace.*[1]

Johnson uses the definite article in a number of other ways
very similar to this 'generic' use. For example:

> At once is lost the pride of aweful state,
> The golden canopy, the glitt'ring plate,
> The regal palace, the luxurious board,
> The liv'ried army, and the menial lord.[2]

There is no rhetorical device which gives Johnson greater
help in the attainment of that 'grandeur of generality' to
which he aspired:

> The festal blazes, the triumphal show,
> The ravish'd standard, and the captive foe,
> The senate's thanks, the gazette's pompous tale,
> With force resistless o'er the brave prevail.[3]

What could be simpler? *The* + generalized adjective + generic noun. Yet the result is poetry of no mean order.

With the same object of impressing on the reader the
abundance and irrefutability of the evidence Johnson makes
telling use of schematic figures based on parallelism and
repetition. These vary from the simple repetition in lines
25-26—

> For gold his sword the hireling ruffian draws,
> For gold the hireling judge distorts the laws

—through the more extended repetition of 'him' and 'his' in
the passage about Wolsey[4] to the skilful rhetoric of the
closing lines:

> For love, which scarce collective man can fill;
> For patience sov'reign o'er transmuted ill;
> For faith, that panting for a happier seat,
> Counts death kind Nature's signal of retreat:

---

[1] ll. 32, 33, 37, 47, 48, 166, 170. Again:
> How rarely reason guides the stubborn choice,
> Rules the bold hand, or prompts the suppliant voice.   (ll. 11–12.)

And again:
> Dart the quick taunt, and edge the piercing gibe.   (l. 62.)

[2] ll. 113–16.   [3] ll. 175–8.

[4] Quoted on p. 139 above.

> These goods for man the laws of heav'n ordain,
> These goods he grants, who grants the pow'r to gain;
> With these celestial wisdom calms the mind,
> And makes the happiness she does not find.

Such passages suggest that excessive emphasis is often placed on the part played by the couplet in the rhetoric of Augustan verse. In *The Vanity of Human Wishes* it is not the couplet but the verse-paragraph that is the basic unit of composition.[1] Like Pope in the best parts of the *Essay on Man* Johnson here succeeded in weaving his end-stopped couplets into a larger unity. The irresistible march of the lines forms a fitting accompaniment to the massive accumulation of sombre statements about life and bears witness to his rhetorical skill.

III

Like the Idea of Tragedy and Comedy, the Idea of Horatian and Juvenalian Satire acted as an inspiration to poets; it provided masks, bearing, and gesture which enabled them to express their deepest feelings within the necessary cloak of stylization. It is fitting that the great age of verse satire in England should have drawn to a close with a poem in which the greatest man of letters of the century found in Juvenal as perfect a model as the greatest poet of the period had found in Horace.[2]

Yet Johnson's debt to Juvenal should not blind us to the originality of his achievement. 'The general character of this translation', he remarked of the version of Juvenal by Dryden and his associates, 'will be given when it is said to preserve the wit, but to want the dignity of the original. The peculiarity of Juvenal is a mixture of gaiety and stateliness, of

---

[1] Johnson told Boswell that he composed 'walking up and down in [his] room', with 'perhaps fifty [lines] at a time' in his head (*Life*, ii. 15). Another master of the verse-paragraph, Milton, seems often to have composed in the same way.

[2] Boswell noticed the coincidence that Johnson's earlier Juvenalian satire, *London*, was published at the same time as Pope's *One Thousand Seven Hundred and Thirty Eight*, 'so that England had at once its Juvenal and Horace as poetical monitors' : *Life*, i. 127.

pointed sentences, and declamatory grandeur. His points
have not been neglected; but his grandeur none of the band
seemed to consider as necessary to be imitated, except
Creech.'[1] Johnson took for his model one of the most sombre
of Juvenal's satires, and the quality which he was most
concerned to reproduce was not the wit of his original but
its grandeur. In spite of the wish that Democritus would
revisit the world and improve it 'With chearful wisdom and
instructive mirth',[2] there is even less humour in Johnson's
poem than in Juvenal's. In his hands the Juvenalian satire
became a sermon of incomparable weight and authority.

It is hard to see how the old fallacy that the eighteenth
century was an age of facile optimism could have survived
a reading of Johnson's 'tragical satire', which is not only
deeply pessimistic, but pessimistic in an almost medieval
way. In tone it has a manifest affinity to the tradition of
contemptus mundi, while the lesson it enforces is the lesson
of Erasmus in *The Praise of Folly*:

Were any one plac'd on that Tower, from whence *Jove* is fancied by
the Poets to Survey the World, he would all around discern how many
Grievances and Calamities our whole Life is on every Side encompassed
with: How Unclean our Birth, how Troublesome our Tendance in
the Cradle, how liable our Childhood is to a Thousand Misfortunes,
how Toilsome and full of Drudgery our Riper Years, how Heavy
and Uncomfortable our Old Age, and lastly, how Unwelcome the
Unavoidableness of Death. Farther, in every Course of Life how many
Wracks there may be of torturing Diseases, how many unhappy
Accidents may casually occurr, how many unexpected Disasters may
arise, and what strange Alterations may one Moment produce? Not to
mention such Miseries as Men are mutually the Cause of, as Poverty,
Imprisonment, Slander, Reproach, Revenge, Treachery, Malice,
Cousenage, Deceit, and so many more, as to reckon them all would be
as puzz'ling Arithmetick as the numbring of the Sands.[3]

---

[1] *Lives*, i. 447. [2] l. 50.
[3] *Moriæ Encomium: or, A Panegyrick upon Folly . . . Done into English* (1709), pp. 47–48.
In this chapter and elsewhere I am indebted to Dr. F. R. Leavis's stimulating and
provocative book *Revaluation* (1936).

IX

'PROPER LANGUAGE':
SOME CONCLUSIONS

Rapin does further remark, That there is a particular Rhetorick
for Poetry, *which the* Modern Poets *scarce understand at all*.[1]

Two courses are open to the critic who sets out to
recommend Augustan poetry. One is to emphasize
the variety of the poetic modes practised in the
period, with particular mention of such poems as Dryden's
Fables, Prior's *vers de société*, the *Elegy to the Memory of an
Unfortunate Lady*, and *Elegy Wrote in a Country Church Yard*
—poems which seldom fail in their appeal even with readers
who have little taste for the eighteenth century. Although
this line of argument is valid and important, I have taken
the other, that of pointing to the richness and variety of
conception and idiom that may be found within what is
usually regarded as a single poetic mode: Augustan satirical
verse. When Mr. C. S. Lewis repeats the notion that 'the
monotony of Augustan satire . . . is easily felt',[2] is he really
calling to mind the masterpieces of the period, *Hudibras*,
MacFlecknoe, *The Rape of the Lock*? If he were, it would
occur to him that just as 'under the common name of allegory
things of quite different natures are concealed',[3] so the term
satire covers poems of many different sorts.

The first step towards an understanding of Augustan
satire is to realize that it is not, in the specialized sense, a
poetic 'kind'. It is a temper of writing, unsusceptible of any
but a very wide definition, which may find an outlet in any
of a number of different kinds and in correspondingly
diverse styles. *Absalom and Achitophel*, the *Imitations of
Horace* and *The Vanity of Human Wishes* are all—to adopt
Johnson's definition of satire—'poems in which wickedness
or folly is censured', and they were all known as satires in

---

[1] Sir Thomas Pope Blount, *De Re Poetica: or, Remarks upon Poetry* (1694), p. 30.
[2] *The Allegory of Love* (ed. of 1938), p. 232.　　　　[3] Ibid., p. 234.

their own age. Yet they differ greatly in nature. *Absalom and Achitophel* is a heroic or 'historical' poem, shot through with wit and irony, describing the progress of a political plot, the *Imitations of Horace* are familiar studies of contemporary abuses and follies, while *The Vanity of Human Wishes* is a formal indictment of human folly. The style and arrangement of the poems vary according to their conception. *Absalom and Achitophel* follows a narrative arrangement and is written in an elevated heroic idiom; the *Imitations of Horace* reproduce the familiar idiom as well as the apparently casual form of their original; while *The Vanity of Human Wishes*, avoiding equally the familiar details and the informality of Horatian satire, exhibits the *ordonnance* and the high style of an elevated sermon. The basic difference of conception has its effect on every aspect of the poet's art—versification, diction, and imagery.

For this reason all generalizations about Augustan satire, or about Augustan poetry in general, which ignore differences of intention and kind are likely to be invalid. The threadbare topic of 'poetic diction', for example, cannot intelligently be discussed in general terms. As a critic remarked in 1738, 'to form an exact judgment of poetic diction, we ought to consider the several kinds of poetry apart; for each requires a very different manner of expression'.[1] The critics responsible for the recent revival of interest in the nature poetry of the eighteenth century have necessarily paid a great deal of attention to the question of 'poetic diction'.[2] Mr. C. V. Deane and others have rightly stressed the difference between the use of a formalized diction to achieve effects not otherwise obtainable and the lazy use of it for no good purpose.[3] Yet this discussion has

---

[1] *Observations on Poetry, Especially the Epic: Occasioned by the Late Poem upon Leonidas* [by H. Pemberton], p. 98.

[2] It is, I think, too late to protest against the use of the phrase 'poetic diction' in the specialized sense of the formalized descriptive idiom used by many eighteenth-century poets. It is very misleading, however; particularly because it is a question-begging term suggestive of an appliqué. When such phrases were successfully used they formed an organic part of the whole idiom of a poem.

[3] See in particular *Aspects of Eighteenth Century Nature Poetry* (1935), by C. V. Deane;

tended to concentrate attention on minor poetry. The critical misdirection for which Wordsworth is largely responsible has not been altogether put right: 'poetic diction' still looms like a thundercloud over the critic who seeks to interest modern readers in the poetry of the eighteenth century. But it is primarily in descriptive poetry that 'poetic diction' is prominent; and since descriptive poetry is not the heart of the Augustan achievement, it is unjust and highly misleading to begin a discussion of Pope or Augustan verse in general by discussing the merits and limitations of this specialized diction. It is not by Pope's *Pastorals* and *Windsor Forest* that he himself is to be judged, or the age that produced him, but by such mature works as the *Imitations of Horace*; and they, as W. P. Ker pointed out many years ago, resemble *Absalom and Achitophel* in being 'perfectly free' from 'poetic diction'.[1] It was not Pope but the 'pre-Romantic' Gray who remarked that 'the language of the age is never the language of poetry'.[2] Pope would no more have assented to this than Dryden. His first comment would have been that such a generalization *could not* be true, because each species of poetry has its own 'language', its own measure of acceptance and rejection, its own variations from and adherence to 'the real language of men'.[3]

Particularly false is the notion that Augustan poets were unwilling to 'call a spade a spade'. If Pope used so many ingenious periphrases for 'scissors' in *The Rape of the Lock*, he had the best of reasons for it.[4] Neither he nor any reputable

two essays in *Essays in Criticism and Research* (1942), by G. Tillotson; and *The Language of Natural Description in Eighteenth-Century Poetry* (1949), by John Arthos.

[1] *Form and Style in Poetry* (1928), p. 167.

[2] *Correspondence*, ed. Toynbee and Whibley (1935), i. 192. It is unlikely that Gray would have committed himself to this statement in an essay designed for publication. Read in its context it is the stimulating but one-sided remark of a practising poet: taken in isolation it is the worst sort of *a priori* theorizing. Any generalization about poetry which excludes in a phrase the whole of French poetry ('whose verse, where the thought or image does not support it, differs in nothing from prose') stands self-condemned.

[3] Wordsworth's phrase. It may seem odd to mention 'poetic diction' in the concluding chapter of a study where it has made so few earlier appearances. But it is the fact that I have had occasion to refer to the subject so seldom that is significant.

[4] See p. 89, above.

Augustan poet had the slightest hesitation in using familiar words in his verse, so long as decorum was not violated. On the contrary they produced a new class of poetry, inspired by the *Eclogues* of Virgil, of which the whole effect consisted, as Warton pointed out, 'in describing the objects as they really exist in life, like Hogarth's paintings, without heightening or enlarging them, and without adding any imaginary circumstances'.[1] These poems, which include Gay's *Trivia*, some of the descriptive parts of *The Rape of the Lock*, and several of Swift's poems (notably the descriptions of *A City Shower* and *The Morning*, and the lines on his own death), display a mastery of the material and diction of every day for which one may search in vain in later English poetry.

The abstractions and personifications in Augustan verse which have annoyed so many critics are no more to be understood without reference to decorum than is the use of 'poetic diction'. The question to be asked is not 'Are abstractions and personifications legitimate in poetry?' but 'Is this a good poem?' When this empirical approach is adopted, with specific poems and passages on the table for examination, it becomes clear that in moralizing verse, in particular, abstractions suited the temper of the age. When they were handled by a poet of genius, as in *The Vanity of Human Wishes*, *a priori* justification becomes an impertinence. Numerous examples of the clusters of abstractions and personifications which may be found in the more elevated passages of Pope and Johnson have been pointed out and examined in the preceding pages.

At a time when enthusiasm for Jacobean drama and Metaphysical poetry has induced many critics to suggest that imagery is the very heart of poetry, the accusation that Augustan verse is undistinguished in the realm of metaphor and simile is potentially more damaging than even its supposed reliance on 'poetic diction'. This charge has been made not only by those primarily interested in modern poetry, like Mr. Macneice, but also by a scholar as

---

[1] *Essay*, ii. 51–52.

distinguished as Mr. F. W. Bateson.[1] But it should be obvious that the 'absence of metaphor' of which Mr. Bateson complains is characteristic (at the most) only of some poetic kinds, and of the work of minor rather than major poets. Why should the Augustan age, alone in the annals of our literature, be fated to condemnation on the evidence of its inferior work?

It has become clear in the course of this study that the imagery of a poem, like the diction or the versification, must be considered in its relation to the total intention of the poet and the characteristics of the kind he is practising. Why does *Absalom and Achitophel* contain far less imagery than *Annus Mirabilis*? Not because Dryden decided, as he matured, that imagery was to be avoided. If that were the reason, the difficulties which many critics have found in accounting for the Donne-like imagery of *Eleonora* and other of the complimentary poems which Dryden wrote towards the end of his career, long after he had 'settled his system of propriety',[2] would be very real. The true significance of the difference is more limited and more interesting. Dryden learned that the best way to write a narrative in a heroic or near-heroic style involved a more sparing use of imagery. In many other kinds his use of imagery did not diminish from first to last. Similarly (if I may use for illustration two poems outside the scope of this book as a whole), a comparison of the *Essay on Criticism* and the *Essay on Man* shows that while the earlier poem has frequent witty images, the later concentrates on neat, schematic figures. Does this mean that Pope's development brought with it a sparser and drier use of metaphors and similes? If so, how are we to account for the last Book of *The Dunciad*, which is richer in imagery than anything he wrote at any other time? The explanation is again one of decorum. The *Essay on Man* is a poem on a more serious subject than the *Essay on Criticism*: its model is rather the 'grave march' of Lucretius than 'the gaieties of Horace':[3]

---

[1] *Modern Poetry* (1938), p. 97; *English Poetry and the English Language* (1934), p. 58.
[2] Johnson's *Lives*, i. 435.
[3] *E.-C.*, vii. 324–5.

the style is accordingly more elevated, and less witty. Satirical poetry, on the other hand, is usually hospitable to witty imagery. When in *The Art of Sinking* Pope counsels those who wish to write bad poetry to use many images, and to draw them 'from the lowest things, which is a certain way to sink the highest',[1] he is talking of elevated verse. Such images are essential to the idiom of his own satirical verse, as may be seen on any page of the *Imitations of Horace* or *The Dunciad.*

One reason for the belief that Augustan verse is impoverished in imagery has been a serious misunderstanding not only of the theories of the poets of the period, but even more of the views of the leading philosophers and scientists as represented by the Royal Society. It is often supposed that they distrusted metaphors and similes so much that they wished to banish them from the language of poetry. The statements that have led to this belief are not numerous (suspiciously few are habitually quoted, and these in a manner which sometimes argues little acquaintance with the contexts in which they occur), and they come readily to mind. The passage in which Sprat censures 'this trick of *Metaphors*'[2] has been quoted a hundred times. But he is describing the style demanded of members of the Royal Society in their scientific reports. Is there any reliable evidence that he himself, or the Society as a whole, wished to deprive poetry of its traditional imagery?

In fact the evidence points the opposite way. In a passage so important that it demands extensive quotation Sprat argues that the discoveries of the Society, far from being hostile to 'wits' and writers, will be of the greatest use to them:

To this purpose [he remarks] I must premise, that it is requir'd in the best, and most delightful *Wit*; that it be founded on such images which are generally known, and are able to bring a strong, and a sensible impression on the *mind*. The several subjects from which it has bin rays'd in all Times, are the *Fables*, and *Religions* of the *Antients*, the

[1] Ch. x.   [2] Spingarn, ii. 117.

Civil Histories of all Countries, the *Customs of Nations*, the *Bible*, the *Sciences*, and *Manners of Men*, the several *Arts* of their hands, and the works of *Nature*. In all these, where there may be a resemblance of one thing to another, as there may be in all, there is a sufficient Foundation for *Wit*. This in all its kinds has its increases, heigths, and decays, as well as all other human things: Let us then examin what Parts of it are already exhausted, and what remain new, and untouch'd, and are still likely to be farther advanc'd.[1]

After a most interesting discussion of the principal sources of metaphors and similes Sprat uses the example of Bacon to recommend images from experimental philosophy:

This excellent Writer [he says triumphantly] was abundantly recompenc'd for his Noble Labors in that *Philosophy*, by a vast Treasure of admirable *Imaginations* which it afforded him, wherewith to express and adorn his thoughts about other matters. I will not confine this *Observation* to one single *Author* [he goes on], though he was one of the first and most artificial Managers of this way of *Wit*. I will venture to declare in general of the *English Tongue*, That as it contains a greater stock of *Natural* and *Mechanical Discoveries*, so it is also more inrich'd with beautiful *Conceptions*, and inimitable *Similitudes*, gather'd from the *Arts* of mens hands, and the *Works of Nature*, than ever any other *Language* could produce.[2]

It is perfectly clear that Sprat's attitude to the imagery of poetry is in no way hostile; his position is that of Hobbes, as stated in his *Answer* to Davenant's *Preface to Gondibert*:

From *Knowing much*, proceedeth the admirable variety and novelty of Metaphors and Similitudes, which are not possible to be lighted on in the compass of a narrow knowledge. And the want whereof compelleth a Writer to expressions that are either defac'd by time or sullied with vulgar or long use. For the Phrases of Poesy, as the airs of musick, with often hearing become insipide, the Reader having no more sense of their force then our Flesh is sensible of the bones that sustain it. As the sense we have of bodies consisteth in change and variety of impression, so also does the sense of language in the variety and changeable use of words. I mean not in the affectation of words newly brought home from travail, but in new and with all significant

---

[1] *History*, p. 413.   [2] Ibid., pp. 416–17.

translation to our purposes of those that be already received, and in far fetch't but withal apt, instructive, and comly similitudes.[1]

This would be more suitable as a defence of 'Metaphysical' poetry than as a prologue to an age in which poetry is supposed to be deprived of its heredity of figured language. There were, indeed, minor disagreements. Davenant favoured images 'of any Science, as well mechanicall as liberall',[2] while Hobbes considered the use of imagery from 'humble or evil arts' to be one of the 'Indecencies of an Heroick Poem'.[3] But this was a specialized disagreement about heroic decorum.[4] Neither here nor in any other responsible critical essay was the view expressed that poetry should go bare of imagery. There were extremists in the Royal Society, as there are anywhere else; but the great majority of the Society would have been astonished at the relentless hostility to figurative language in verse which has so often been attributed to them since.

One further passage may be quoted, this time from a critic writing during Pope's lifetime. It is of interest not only because it shows a particularly clear awareness of the importance of decorum in imagery, but also because it seems to have been written with a retrospective glance at the passage from Sprat quoted above.

On this Head our Moderns seem to excel the Ancients [wrote Joseph Trapp], and to have found out an Use of Comparisons which they were utter Strangers to. Theirs are merely ornamental; ours often contain the Points of Epigram, the Jibes of Satire, and the Banters of Comedy; an Art which *Ovid, Martial, Juvenal, Horace* and *Terence* knew very little of. . . . 'Tis true, Tragic and Epic Poets ought totally to avoid these witty Allusions; which are below the Severity of their Style, and the Dignity of their Compositions. The Comparisons that serve for Illustration only, come within their Province; such as we meet with very frequently in *Homer* and *Virgil*: Tho' (to say the Truth) even the best Writers among the Ancients seem on this Head to labour under

[1] Spingarn, ii. 65.   [2] Ibid. 26.
[3] Ibid. 64.
[4] Dryden abandoned Davenant's side for that of Hobbes between *Annus Mirabilis* and his translation of *Virgil*.

a Poverty of Matter. In the Description of a Battle, for Instance, the Similes of a Lion, a Bull, a Serpent, an Eagle, and other Animals of the fiercer Kind, recur too frequently under some small Variations. But in After-Ages the Increase of Arts, and Sciences, and of Religion more particularly, open'd a new Field, which has minister'd abundantly not only to the Emolument of Mankind in general, but in this, and in all other Respects, to the Refinement of Wit.[1]

Modern critics believe that the imagery of Augustan poetry is commonplace, and attribute this to the New Science: Trapp uses the same influence to explain an opposite diagnosis. The contradiction is complete. The only way out of the difficulty is to lay aside preconceptions about Cartesianism and poetry and examine some of the best poetry written in the Augustan age empirically and 'candidly'. Then one finds that while there is a dearth of successful imagery in some Augustan poetic modes, others— notably the satiric modes examined in this study—exhibit imagery as powerful and as well adapted to its purpose as that in any other period of our literature. It is partly because such overworked topics as the evolution of the heroic couplet and eighteenth-century 'poetic diction' have distracted attention from the imagery of Augustan satire that the relation of the best work of Butler, Dryden, and Pope to earlier English poetry has seldom been adequately understood. To notice how slight the alterations are which Pope made in the imagery of Donne's satires when he 'versifyed' them, and how close is the relation between many of the images he retained and those in *Piers Plowman*, is to understand once for all that the great Augustans are poets writing full in the English tradition.[2]

The real influence of the New Science is to be found in the realistic bent of literature throughout our period. It was not imagery that poets lacked, but tales to tell. Poets have always done much of their work obliquely; but 'the delightful deceit of *Fables*' was deeply distrusted by the scientists,

---

[1] pp. 137-8.
[2] I have examined Pope's adaptations from Donne in detail in 'Pope and "The Weighty Bullion of Dr. Donne's Satires"' (*P.M.L.A.*, Dec. 1951).

and this distrust began to undermine the foundations of many species of poetry, notably the Heroic Poem. Mythological beings of all sorts were the type of these fictions:

The *Poets* began of old to impose the deceit. They to make all things look more venerable than they were, devis'd a Thousand false *Chimaeras*; on every *Field*, *River*, *Grove*, and *Cave*, they bestow'd a *Fantasm* of their own making: With these they amaz'd the world; these they cloath'd with what shapes they pleas'd; by these they pretended, that all Wars, and Counsels, and Actions of men were administred. And in the modern *Ages* these *Fantastical Forms* were reviv'd and possess'd *Christendom*, in the very height of the *Scholemens* time: An infinit number of *Fairies* haunted every house; all Churches were fill'd with *Apparitions*; men began to be frighted from their *Cradles*, which fright continu'd to their *Graves*, and their Names also were made the causes of scaring others. . . . But from the time in which the *Real Philosophy* has appear'd there is scarce any whisper remaining of such *horrors*: Every man is unshaken at those Tales at which his *Ancestors* trembled: The cours of things goes quietly along, in its own true channel of *Natural Causes* and *Effects*.[1]

The line from this passage to Johnson's censure of *Lycidas* is sufficiently clear.[2]

The difficulty about subjects for poetry is so fundamental in this period that it is interesting to note Sprat's advice. It occurs in one of the multitude of discussions of the true nature of 'wit' which appeared throughout the Augustan age.

The true *Raillery* [Sprat wrote] should be a defence for *Good* and *Virtuous* Works, and should only intend the derision of extravagant, and the disgrace of vile and dishonourable things. This kind of *Wit* ought to have the nature of *Salt*, to which it is usually compar'd; which preserves and keeps sweet the good, and the sound parts of all Bodies, and only frets, dries up, and destroys those humors which putrify and corrupt.[3]

What Sprat is demanding is simply Augustan satire.

The importance of Dryden is evident. He confirmed the view that contemporary life was the best subject for an

---

[1] Sprat's *History*, p. 340.
[2] 'What we have gotten by this revolution, you will say, is a great deal of good sense. What we have lost, is a world of fine fabling.' Hurd's *Letters on Chivalry and Romance*, ed. Morley, p. 154.   [3] *History*, p. 419. Cf. Shaftesbury's view that ridicule is the test of truth.

Augustan poet. In *Annus Mirabilis* he made a bold effort to use the manner of *Gondibert* for describing two important happenings of the day. In *Absalom and Achitophel*, his skill immensely increased by long dramatic training, he brilliantly avoided the humourlessness which is the besetting fault of the earlier poem and found the solution to his problem. In doing so he marked out the true direction for Augustan poetry.

Implicit in the discovery that contemporary life was the best field for the Augustan poet was the discovery that the satiric must be one of the principal modes of his vision. Satire is seldom concerned with the distant, the vaguely descried—these are the natural prerogative of Romance; its true quarry is to be found nearer at hand, in the things that go on all around one day after day. From *Hudibras* to the middle of the eighteenth century such subject-matter and such a mode of vision are central to the course of English poetry. Hence the unpopularity of the period with a Romantic generation: hence its growing esteem at a time when Donne remains high in favour.

The old accusation that the poetry of this period is artificial and conventional has little force. If it means that Augustan poetry deals with the life of a time when manners were artificial compared with those of today we may give a limited assent; merely remembering that what seems natural to us will seem conventional to our descendants. But if it means that the Augustan poets relied on poetic conventions more heavily than those of other ages it is highly disputable. The poetry of Dryden, Pope, and Johnson is hardly more 'conventional' than that of Chaucer, Spenser, or Milton. It may even be doubted if it is in any true sense more conventional than the poetry of Donne. It is conventional simply because it was written by men living in the last age of the Renaissance, who had still a framework of critical theory to afford them guidance. This theory had important bearings on the poet's choice of metre, diction, and imagery. Later poets have been the poorer for its disappearance.

INDEX

References to the Preface are not listed

Abbott, C. C. 2 n.

'Absalom': 56, 64–66.

Achilles: 79, 81, 94.

'Achitophel': *see* Shaftesbury, 1st Earl of.

Addison, J. Wrote Latin verse, 11; his opinion of *Hudibras*, 21; quoted on Virgil's *Georgics*, 78 n.; Pope's lines on, 109.

'admiration': 83.

Arber's *English Garner* : quoted, 29, 33.

Ariosto, L. Contrasted with Butler, 23–24; satirized by Butler, 26.

Aristotle: as a rhetorician, 8.

Arnall, W. In *The Dunciad*, 123.

Arthos, J. *The Language of Natural Description in Eighteenth-Century Poetry*, 148 n.

Aubrey, J. *Brief Lives* quoted, 35 n.

Augustus: 114.

Ayres, P. His translation of *Le Comte de Gabalis*, 80 n.

Bacon, Francis: and Butler, 26 n., 31; his imagery commended by Sprat, 152.

Barclay, Alexander: *The Ship of Fools*, 18.

Barclay, John: *Argenis* quoted, 54, 74–75 n.; *Euphormio*, 54 n.

'Barzillai' in *Absalom and Achitophel*, 66–67.

Bateson, F. W. 99 n.; on Pope's *Moral Essays*, 112 n.; *English Poetry and the English Language*, 150.

Bathurst, Allen, Earl Bathurst: surprised about Pope's third *Moral Essay*, 112 n.

Bayes, in *The Rehearsal*: Theobald's role in *The Dunciad* resembles that of Bayes, 117.

Bayle, P. Quoted on the Rosicrucians, 80.

Behmen, J. 28.

Bentley, R. His speech in *The Dunciad* quoted, 128.

Bethel, Slingsby: 69–70.

Blackmore, Sir Richard: Pope's lines on quoted, 45; Preface to *Alfred* quoted, 95.

Blast upon Bays, A: quoted, 124.

Blount, Sir Thomas Pope: *De Re Poetica*, 6 n., quoted 146.

Boileau, N. 1 n.; Pope imitates, 11 n.; 'Dissertation sur Joconde' quoted, 43; his attitude to Scarron, 44; as satirist, 101, 109 n.; *Le Lutrin* praised by Dryden, 44–45, 47–48, 49; and *The Rape of the Lock*, 77, 80, 84 n., 85, 89, 95; and *The Dunciad*, 117.

Bolingbroke, Viscount (Henry St. John): recommends Horace to Pope as a model, 103; Pope's apostrophe to quoted, 105; and *The New Dunciad*, 121–2.

Bond, R. P. *English Burlesque Poetry 1700–1750*, 20 n., 88 n.

Bossu, R. Le: *A General View of the Epick Poem* quoted, x, 71, 79, 81, 83 n.

Boswell, J. Cibber's resemblance to, 123; *Life of Johnson* quoted, 137 n., 144 nn.

Bradner, L. *Musae Anglicanae*, 11 n., 58 n.; 'Poems on the Defeat of the Spanish Armada', 58 n.

Brome, R. Cites Eustathius in Pope's *Odyssey*, 82 n.

Bronson, B. H. 'Personification Reconsidered', 141 n.

Brooks, H. F. Thesis on Oldham quoted, 11 n.

Brower, R. A. 'Dryden's Epic Manner', 59 n.

Brown, J. *Essay on Satire*, 137 n.

Browne, Sir George: Pope's lines on 'Sir Plume' quoted and discussed, 87–88 & n.; 93 n.; 131.

Buckingham, 2nd Duke of (George Villiers): 'Zimri', 69; Pope's description of his death quoted, 109.

'burlesque': 25, 26 n., 129.

Burnet, Gilbert (Bishop of Salisbury): recommends Juvenal and Persius, 136.

PRINTED IN GREAT BRITAIN
AT THE UNIVERSITY PRESS, OXFORD
BY VIVIAN RIDLER
PRINTER TO THE UNIVERSITY